Refusing To Learn

Really, How Dumb
Do You Think
I Am

Refusing to Learn
Really, How Dumb Do You Think I Am?

Refusing to Learn
Really, How Dumb Do You Think I Am?

ISBN: 13: 979-8717020404
IMPRINT: Indie Publishing

Printed in the United States of America
10 9 8 7 6 5 4 3 2 1

Refusing to Learn
Really, How Dumb Do You Think I Am?

by
Brian C. McGuire
Towson University

FAR-LEFT PUBLICATIONS

Brian C. McGuire

Refusing to Learn
Really, How Dumb Do You Think I Am?

Brian C. McGuire was born in Baltimore, Maryland on May 31, 1970. He spent thirteen years serving in the United States Armed Forces. He received a Bachelor of Science from Towson University. His areas of research interests include the mental terrain of Community Psychology: A field of Human Services that places special emphasis on problems associated with urban groups and how they adapt under low socioeconomic conditions during childhood, adolescence, and throughout the course of adult development and aging, and sociocultural influences (including theoretical concepts pertaining to how various dimensions of culture influence stress and coping). Brian is also the author of these exceptional indie reference books: The Ignoble Paradox of Man, The Great Divide: The Social and Cultural Context of Inequality, and The Color of Our Souls: How Multigenerational Experiences Impact Our Lives.

TABLE OF CONTENTS

On Refusing To Learn
Prologue

Refusing To Learn
Introduction

Really, How Dumb Do You Think I Am
Chapter 1

Behind The Government's Deceit
Chapter 2

The Problem With Having An Ascribed Identity
Chapter 3

The Search For An Avowed Identity
Chapter 4

An Identity Crisis Or A Political Stance
Chapter 5

In The Age Of Consciousness
Chapter 6

Arriving At Your True Identity
Chapter 7

Your Essential Self
Epilogue

Dedication

Refusing to Learn: Really, How Dumb Do You Think I Am, is dedicated to young Black males, many of whom want to learn but not from their oppressors. Those who refuse to model themselves after dominant Whites more often drop out of society in search of their own identity. Many of these young brothers struggle to achieve competence. They more often endure great hardship through a trial-and-error adjustment process called creative maladjustment. Unless we can stop, reflect, and redirect their intellectual energy to an intensity that connects them to a better standard of commitment, there is little chance of improving serious disagreements that disrupts good relationships. Might this book be added to a now classic collection of nonfiction literature that attempt to address the difficult or dangerous situation young Black males find themselves in and from which there is no clear or easy way out. Let this book serve as a requisite to healthy intergroup relationships.

Acknowledgements

Writing this book has been both inspiring and challenging. I literally wrote on a topic I overlooked most of my life, a topic that has always been a part of who I am. The entire process left me mentally exhausted. But, I could not have completed it without the valuable assistance of people who knew a great deal and provided extraordinarily perceptive and critical feedback, edited various sections, provided relevant information and, on occasion, offered new insight that helped me create content for various chapters. Today, I thank them all!

As always, I am deeply appreciative of Yvonne M. Drake. Her love and encouragement inspire my confidence and will to continue writing in the most doubtful or darkest moments.

I am deeply in debt to Anita L. Opher. Her brilliance in the editing of this book was absolutely genius. Needless to say, she was also the reason for writing this book; it was her idea! Without her exceptional intelligence and vision, this book would not exist.

I'd also like to thank Kendra Rhodes for her continuous encouragement in the writing process of this latest book. She's been a great inspiration to me. She's also been the driving force behind the new development.

And finally, I'd like to give my deepest gratitude to Tameika Trent. She's taken time out of her busy schedule to aid me in the marketing and promotion of this and other books. The energy she exerts in getting it done is, without exception, the best. She is always appreciated.

I appreciate them all.

Prologue
On Refusing To Learn

We must never adjust ourselves to economic conditions that take necessities from the many to give luxuries to the few.

Reverend Martin Luther King, Jr., DD (September 1967)

This prologue, On Refusing to Learn, explains what led to the development of this book. You will read in this passage and throughout the book, stories that illustrate many fascinating and varied dimensions of inequality American scholars failed to consider or explain. But first, it is necessary for you to open your mind so we can explore the plight of Black people in broader cultural dimensions.

This book is not a cure-all for our inhumanity toward other people. But, it does look at one knotty problem scholars refuse to address as if to say it's unresolveable. In this way, they contribute enormously to the problem of why so many young Black males aren't adjusting well in American society. It also looks at why many behave the way they do. And last, this book considers how young Black males can learn to cope more effectively in their daily lives. I am enthusiastic about this book's potential to improve your understanding of inequality as we are well into the new millennium. It is truly an exciting topic of discovery for me.

To a degree, the literature in this book will strike you as being simple and common sense. However, it will uncover the unexpected in Black behavior. For example, it may appear obvious to many that young Black males struggle in grade school due to mental and physical health deficiencies. After all, refusing to learn is a sign of social maladjustment. However, scholars found that refusing to learn may have more to do with cultural attitudes rather than Black males having a genetic disposition.

As you gathered thus far, this book does not make assumptions about Black people at face value however reasonable it may sound to you. In fact, it draws reasonable conclusions after rigorously testing assumptions that appear true. Refusing to Learn: Really, How Dumb Do You Think I Am, is a scholarly reference book that draws from many academic disciplines to observe, describe, and explain the behavior of young Black males in their refusing to learn.

To test the book's validity, you can check to see if it, at any point in time, ever described the attitude and behavior of any Blacks you may know, not just young Black males. For example, you may choose to ask a neighbor, discuss it with your friends, or call on a relative to answer your questions. As well, context is an important dimension of this book. Contexts create circumstances that form the environment within which people exists or events take place. Without reference to context, the problem of inequality cannot be fully understood.

As American culture continues to change, we need to address new problems in proper context, such as national diversity, global interdependence, as well as women and their roles in American society. As you read this book, you will realize that it considers the influence context has on young Black males and their perceptions. You may even become more sensitive to Black people and how the circumstances that form their environment influence their perceptions.

The Reason For
Writing This Book

I came across the idea to write this book after developing my third book title, The Color of Our Souls. It was inspired by chapter 7, Refusing to Learn, a phrase I stumbled onto while conducting Internet-based search on the topic. It would be my first attempt to address an important topic not quite taboo but one most people refuse to consider because of social or cultural prohibitions. This book, Refusing to Learn: Really, How Dumb Do You think I Am, is my attempt to fully address the daily problems young Black males endure who refuse to receive formal education under a system of oppression.

Refusing to Learn is a worthwhile read. I try to capture the exact circumstances of Black people in this book. Readers will fully appreciate the material covered. Materials are challenging and stimulating despite the lack of awareness on the topic. Various topics in this book are intended to inform people who are unaware of the problem. Each is designed to give you a good idea about what's going on with the mindset of young Black males and what determines their behavioral outlook on life.

It's been awhile since a book of this caliber was dedicated to giving new life or energy to a long-lost topic. Most topical discussions on the matter were seemingly ignored as professionals forgot or failed to continue its disclosure in the public domain. Truth of the matter is those who resist education continuously expose the truth behind this topic by refusing to learn. This book sheds light on that fact.

I'm often inspired to write after reading the efforts and sacrifices made by Foundational Black Americans (FBA). Many of these people were enslaved in Africa and forced to bear labor here in the Americas, most of whom, along with their descendants, built this great nation of ours. Slave rebellions like the ones led by Gabriel Prosser in Virginia in 1800, Benjamin Montgomery, a slave who invented a steamboat propeller designed for shallow waters in the 1850's, and Dr. Daniel Hale Williams, Jr, a medical doctor who conducted the first successful open heart surgery in 1893, are among the many less well-known Black historical figures who motivate me to write. Dr. Daniel Hale Williams, Jr, also founded the first Black-owned hospital in America.

You might say reading critical race topics allow me to explore the deepest and truest nature of humanity. Although there are many historical figures who inspire my writing—with all the protesting occurring over the official murders of young Black Americans—Foundational Black Americans remind me just how far we, as a people, have to come in order to bring about change in America. Allow me to shed more light on this topic.

Many Blacks are reared under the minimal level of subsistence below which people should not be expected to exist. In fact, many are among the working poor who depend on public assistance to stay alive. Their circumstances are more often characterized by hardship or suffering. Many more are affected by circumstances that make it nearly impossible to function productively in American society. Chronic life conditions add stress to their lives while uncontrollable life events affect their circumstances in ways that are often beyond their control.

Further, Whites are often disillusioned about the circumstances of young Black males or Black people, in general, for that matter. For the majority of Americans, the exact circumstances of young Blacks are elusive. So for them—Blacks who understand that their future will not change their position much in life—why should they perform admirably under the circumstances when their best performance will be given at a disadvantage? In fact, they feel like it makes more sense for Black people to separate themselves so that they can come together to create their own cultural mainstream.

Many Whites feel that Black males are maladaptive. They believe that by the time Black males become adults, they turn out to be the world's ideal of unsuccessful or unlucky. They feel that Blacks are destined to repeatedly fail at life. American history teaches them that false belief, an ideal image existing only in their imaginations.

Many are genuinely concerned about the problems young Blacks endured and continue to endure. But American history teaches them that Black people will not avail themselves of opportunities needed to better their circumstances. In fact, they're taught that young Black males contribute to their own plight by lacking in ambition and failing to take chances, especially chances that offer some degree of advantage. One Black scholar offered an explanation.

Reverend Martin Luther King, Jr., DD, believed that what Whites were witnessing in young Black males was an independent approach to problem-solving he called creative maladjustment. Dr. King ascertained the reason why so many young Black males refuse to educate themselves. He understood that it was not about being socially maladjusted to learning. In fact, it was a political stance made to not attain any knowledge under the oppressive conditions set forth by White supremacy. He believed young Black males refused to normalize inequality by becoming functional under a system that continuously expects them to be subservient.

Dr. King also believed that Blacks should never adjust themselves to economic conditions that take what is necessary from the suffering to give that which is desirable but unessential to the few. Dr. King, who was a keynote speaker at an annual conference of the American Psychological Association, marked the significance of how psychologists introduced the concept of social maladjust-ment. He believed that there were certain situations experienced in our lifetime we should never adjust to, alluding to the fact that most people are too well-adjusted to injustice.

King and others worked continuously to expose injustice so that Blacks could rightfully take their place as productive citizens in American society. Nonetheless, it appears that their efforts were not strong enough nor made soon enough to make a difference. Young Black males still refuse to learn. As for Dr. King's effort to unify America—an effort expressed in his famous speech, I Have A Dream—White people continue to display open acts of hatred and hostility toward Black people. A few Whites experience discomfort, uneasiness, and fear in their presence.

In the first half of this prologue, we investigated the reason behind writing this book. We also briefly considered the concept of not-learning based on context. Next, in the introduction, we will officially explore the potential problem behind not-learning, revealing important arguments that addresses the etiology behind it.

Introduction
Refusing To Learn

…wherein people refuse to normalize inequality and work continuously to expose injustice…

Yohuru Williams (October 6, 2017)

Look at them! They refuse to learn! It must be hard work to stay that stupid! How can we teach them when they continue to give into their willful ignorance?

People have various opinions as to why so many Black males are refusing to learn. Some might say the novelty has worn off. At one point in history, the main concern of Blacks was to achieve competency through the use of education. Young and old, freedman and the newly freed, Blacks from every walk of life wanted to experience the power of learning.

After slavery, educating Blacks became a high priority for many educators. Educators from Northern America headed south to setup and establish educational institutions to help Blacks adjust to their new found circumstances. There was quite a bit of resistance against educating Blacks too. Whites—not just from the Southern states but also the Northern states—were adamantly opposed to educating a people who had long been subservient to them. Nevertheless, White resistance never shook the new found conscious state of Black people.

Malcolm little was once told by his teacher that a lawyer was not a realistic goal for a nigger. Instead, he was told to consider becoming a carpenter like Jesus Christ. To set your aspirations on a lower goal can deprive a person of his or her dignity. The loss of pride and self-respect can lead to repeatedly failing at life. In Malcolm's case, he spent 6 years in prison. The loss of ambition had a psychosocial impact on him. He declared his new identity while in prison. Malcolm X would soon emerge as one of the Nation of Islam's greatest intellectuals. How do people learn in the face of overwhelming oppression? Is it even worth learning when it comes at a disadvantage?

It is safe to conclude that *refusing to learn* is a conscious effort to not accept education or information from your oppressors. The concept is based on the understanding that your oppressors will never properly educate you. In fact, it may very well be an intelligent act to not learn under oppressive conditions. The problem is when people openly refuse to educate themselves, important information is lost.

First, there are a few ways you can learn. Learning takes on different connotations for various people. It can be formal or informal, academic or technical, especially vocational or trade, whatever suits the person's best interest. The problem with learning is that society considers what aspect is relevant or irrelevant. Usually, relevancy has to do with what works best for your country. In America, the choice is left up to the individual. Usually, people put their talents to work where they feel it's best needed. When the government removed social structures and community resources from Black America, it relegated them to the lowest levels of civility. Some people believe that relegation was a way to ensure Black people would work low-income jobs forever.

Unfortunately, you do not need an education to work low-income jobs. Thus, many White people believe Blacks would be best suited to work low-income jobs. This, they feel works in the best interest of our great nation. Thus, the question becomes why learn? If our government is trying to keep Black people relegated to a permanent underclass, then why waste your time educating yourself? If the only jobs available for you are at best carpenter and lower income, then educating yourself is a waste of time. Isn't it?

People fail to realize that Blacks are refusing to learn for those very reasons. Today, the dropout rate for young Black males is superseding most identity groups in American society. Many young Blacks are saying they refuse to be educated by a people who oppressed them. They believe that not only are their oppressors purposely miseducating them, but those willing to teach are setting them up for failure.

They learn early on in life that job opportunities are scarce for Black Americans. And, most people are unwilling to give young Black males job opportunities largely due to their racial identity. Either way, the prospect of Blacks attaining gainful employment in a hostile environment looks bleak.

One of the problems is that people believe young Black males are choosing to remain illiterate. They also wonder why so many Blacks are dropping out of grade school, seemingly, without good reason. Some people call it willful ignorance. Whatever the reasoning, most people assume that the feeling of interest or excitement has extinguished for Blacks because education is no longer a new or surprising experience.

But many young Black males say the novelty effect has no bearing on them or their circumstances. They consider it to be an act of insanity to harm or be disloyal to yourself or your people by learning from the very people who subjugated you, especially in the name of White supremacy.

They understand that today's education focuses on Whites or their people, institutions, and cultures, often in a way that is arrogantly dismissive of Black folk. In this regard, many Blacks refuse to normalize inequality by learning in an educational environment, lecture hall, or anywhere where Black people are taught to compromise their intelligence, dignity, or integrity.

Many refuse to educate themselves just to earn a gold-plated watch at retirement. They understand that no amount of education will put them in a position of power in this country. So they refuse to assimilate their ideas and personal gains to help dominant White society by serving in secondary roles that support White production. They feel that today's Blacks are too submissive or eager to follow the wishes of dominant society.

By refusing to learn, they expose the unfair truth behind American Apartheid schools, a system of segregation that gives privileges to those of European origin. Black people feel that true knowledge is forbidden to everyone except people of European origin. In fact, young Blacks believe that the double standard in education comes from having a lack of humanity toward oppressed people. That Black people will never achieve equality under an established social order, especially one regarded as oppressive. Therefore, they believe it is rational for them to consider learning a source of worry, stress, or trouble. And since they can't beat the system and will never truly benefit from it, they are making efforts to search for a new identity.

The Search For A
True Identity

Blacks across the African diaspora are in search of their true identity. Many are returning to their African heritage. And, having respect for African history is part of them redeeming their African heritage. Curiously, Black Americans are also searching for an identity but in hopes of finding one right for them. The problem is they're tired of having their identities ascribed to them.

Having an ascribed identity doesn't always mean taking on the social roles of your oppressors as readily assumed. Nor does it mean returning to your African roots. It more often means being negatively labeled by the people who oppressed you. It's hard to live down cultural stereotypes after having been labeled. The problem is, and has always been, people will develop an oversimplified standardized image of you or your people, customs, or institutions, having been ascribed an identity.

For example, Black males are born under the false belief that they belong to an unambitious people. For this very reason, many Whites ascribe contentment to them. In fact, the more prejudice found in America the greater the chance of Blacks being assigned a negative identity. Such stigmas often saddle them for the remainder of their lives.

The problem Whites have in assigning negative labels to Black people may come from them experiencing conflict between their genuine egalitarian values and their own negative feelings toward the very people they oppressed. Whites also feel emasculated whenever Black people prosper, especially in financial or economical situations. As a result of Black success, Whites more often experience discomfort, uneasiness, and fear. Coupled with the understanding that they may not want Black people to know how it makes them feel, Whites avoid Black people whenever possible. Others resort to aggression. For those reasons, young Black males are making a conscious effort to reject the qualities of dominant society.

In fact, young Black males are making a conscious effort to reject mainstream qualities as a matter of principle. They no longer choose to mimic mainstream fashions and mannerisms such as becoming acculturated or learned in an apparent effort to be socially accepted. Regardless of what the mainstream has to offer, Black males are rejecting any and all success that equates to them acting White thus feminine. As a result, their lives are more often complicated.

Despite complications, many Blacks continue to hold themselves in high regard. Their opinion of themselves is said to come from having a natural ability to adequately cope in the face of overwhelming stress and oppression. So how do they manage to cope when dominant society continues to scold them vigorously and at length for rejecting their ascribed identities? Some managed to create their own cultural mainstream. They learned to successfully negotiate with dominant society through the use of music, art, and other manifestations of the human intellectual achievement. Many others voluntarily withdraw from mainstream society. They more often become preoccupied with maintaining control over their existence.

They struggle to preserve their dignity. They say it is unintelligent for anyone to seek out social acceptance from Whites when the penalty results in more exploitation, oppression, and humiliation of our most vulnerable. For them, the idea of rejecting mainstream qualities is a rational response given by a people who have been pushed to the point when actions must be taken or decisions have to be made. How they come to discover, know, or find the relevance of their own existence complicate matters more. In this way, searching out an identity becomes critical for them.

The Search For An
Avowed Identity

You know the search for awareness is moving in a contrary direction when you're forced to develop your own identity. Black Americans are developing their own names in the search for an avowed identity. It's part of a major effort made by many. In this way, they are assigning names to themselves that sound right or true for them. It's their way of correcting the use of a wrong or unsuitable name or term to describe Black people. It also better characterizes who they are as a whole. The understanding is how do Whites expect Black people to do as well or better than others on the world market using names based on cultural stereotypes? Their premise is simple. They don't!

So then, how come Black Americans refuse to appeal to their Africanism? Many were turned off to the idea of following African tradition. Some were offset by the possibility of modeling themselves after a people who had a falling or failing economy. Others were disturbed over the poor attitudes Africans often display toward Blacks here in America. Still, many Black Americans resisted the notion of Afrocentrism, perhaps, due to a lack of awareness. The only option left for them was to search for their own identity.

Beyond Afrocentrism, there are no such identities as Black names. Black names are made up to sound legitimate for the most part. Today, they are considered to be culture-based identities associated with Black Americans. Assigning Black names to their children and themselves is one way to avow an identity. An avowed identity can consist of names from any major languages: English, European, Hispanic, Arabian, Native American, African, or any language we use separate or in combination. Jamal, Shaquan, and Rakim are prime examples of names that sound right and true for Blacks today. Often, but not always, Black people make up names to characterize an identity they believe to be right or true for them: Key'von, for example. However, you can only combine names in so many ways before you stumble onto names from other cultures. So, Black names are more often found in other cultures. The name Dayvon is inherently Black in the United States but comes from Sanskrit, India, and means powerful warrior.

Another example in searching for your own identity is changing your fashion. You will often see conscious Blacks wear an item of clothing or set of clothes that expresses something positive about their attitude, point of view, or lifestyle. Their clothing usually has connotations that convey grandeur. With them, it is easy to identify their firmness of character, which makes them great or grand and very impressive. They more often have a particular philosophy of life or conception of the world. In many cases, they broaden their worldviews by focusing on resolving problems that affect our most vulnerable. As for young Blacks who are *woke*, their fashion is often commonplace. They dare to be different. The one thing that distinguishes them from everyday, ordinary people is they will not go back to being politically unaware.

Too many Black males focus a great deal of their energy on not-learning. As a result, researchers are realizing that not-learning is an important cognitive ability for gaining independence. We need schools to change curriculums so not-learners can be motivated to learn from every teacher, et cetera.

What We Can Do To Resolve It

What we can do to resolve the problem of not-learning is help Blacks reach full equality. We can accomplish this act by ensuring the rights, treatment, quantity, or values of Black people are characterized by justice, fairness, and impartiality. It's not all about holding public demonstrations but taking other actions to ensure equality. It's not about enduring or showing tolerance, either. It's about America admitting blame and taking responsibility for its mistreatment of private citizens.

Now, all politicians promise to legislate change. This much is true. What we need to do is hold them accountable. We need to request clearly and firmly full equality in a way that is difficult to ignore or deny. We can make sure they meet our demands before we vote for them. Politicians treat Black people as if they are political refugees with no other place to go. If we threaten to change voting priorities, it will gain their attention. In this way, we need to motivate them to make laws or rules designed to bring about equality. We must also hold ourselves accountable in order to function or succeed.

In the introduction, we alerted you to the problem of young Black males who refuse to learn from Whites. In the next chapter, you will read about how young Blacks learn to perceive education. You will also learn the reason why they come to consider Whites with such disdain as we investigate the fascinating mindset of young Black males.

Chapter 1
Really, How Dumb Do You Think I Am

There are some things in our society, some things in our world, to which we should never be adjusted.

Reverend Martin Luther King, Jr., DD (September 1967)

You better back up off of me! Get your hands out of my face! Now, you're talking crazy! I don't like you, either! Really, how dumb do you think I am? Why should Blacks learn anything from their oppressors under the belief they will never be properly educated?

The problem with Western education is the lack of cohesion between teacher and student. Black males understand that they need to be courteous to their teachers. But they're raised in such a way that there needs to be some level of reciprocity or mutual respect. They recognize that people are all the same in terms of humanity. So, when teachers assert their authority, Black students feel like they're violating their sense of pride and self-respect. Most will not allow a teacher to treat them with a lack of respect. That's why there are often teacher-student conflicts that result in many being afraid of Black male students.

What teachers fail to realize is that although their position calls for respect or the honor it deserves, Black children, like everyone else's children, need to have their dignity left in tack. It's the lack of respect that causes pride and esteem issues for them. This situation is why so many young Black males fall into a slippery-slope that takes them down the road to truancy, delinquency and, possibility, criminality.

The reason why Black male students are refusing to learn is threefold. First, young Black males are consciously choosing to not learn if, in fact, learning means assuming a secondary role in today's society. Black males are eager to take their place in society. But, they refuse to take a back seat to dominant White society. Dominant society expects Blacks to be subservient. This means Blacks will never achieve an advantage in society; because, American society was founded on a system of privilege; and, Blacks were never granted special rights or privileges. As a result, Blacks understand that their place, as second class citizens, will be, if it hasn't already been, reduced to a permanent underclass.

The second reason for not-learning is education itself. Today's school systems are segregated. And these segregated schools are designed to keep Black students disadvantaged. If they have to endure a substandard education, then an education truly may not be worth pursuing. In this way, segregation weighs in on the psychological development of Black children, which is the third and final reason why they are refusing to learn. They believe there are some things in life people should never become socially adjusted to. Inequality is one such thing! But before we delve into the actual factuals of refusing to learn, let us first clarify assumptions about it.

It's not that Black males cannot learn. They refuse to learn from White teachers as a matter of principal. White teachers are considered to be part of a system that oppressed Black people. And, they often have the dismissive attitude to go along with it. Many of these teachers would also like Black males to model themselves after them. From their mannerisms to down to their style of dress, they offer themselves as the embodiment of success. The problem is their mannerisms are often viewed as lily-levered. For most Black students, weak and cowardly are hardly good traits to model themselves after. In this way, Black students refuse to learn from a people who they consider cruel and spineless.

When Social Learning
Comes At A Disadvantage

Now, let's begin with an in-depth discussion about why Black male students are refusing to learn. They're often troubled over having to mimic the very people who oppressed them. Doctors, lawyers, even teachers—people normally not thought to be part of an oppressive system—show a lack of moral courage by being mean or cruel to a people who, by the very nature of their existence, are disadvantaged. These are the role models this country teaches everyone to respect. And by that they mean well-educated, fairly affluent White men who are known for their neat, traditional, and often expensive (sophisticated) style of dress.

Well-educated White men are cultured; and, they dress and behave in ways that are not necessarily connected to the standards of masculinity as understood by Black males. Pink shirts, sweaters worn around the neck or waistline, corduroy pants with pants legs worn above the ankle, cute and often colorful socks with symbols on the tubing, and penny loafers (with an actual penny in each shoe) aren't actually fashionable for Black men in the hood.

Most White males are well-spoken. They speak with a particular voice so eloquent and fluent, Black males conventionally think it appropriate for women or girls. There are behavioral patterns associated with their language as well. These gentlemen, preppies during their younger years, have what most people might consider "peculiar" mannerisms.

Black males can readily distinguish differences between their own mannerisms and the way White teachers express their peculiarities. Learning to mimic their patterns of speech and studying their distinctive styles doesn't set well with most Black male students. Black students are turned off to the notion of being subservient to a people who openly admit feeling threatened by their presence. They're also concerned they will become effeminate if they model themselves behind White teachers. After all, it's their mannerisms that Black male students consider to be feminine.

They say it's not their fault that White teachers feel emasculated in the presence of Black males. They understand that there are perceptual differences in attitude that exist between the teacher and student. But, attitudinal differences are the results of environment. And many of these students come from a hostile environment. Curiously, most Black students try not to show an attitude in class. Unfortunately, many teachers become offended over their mannerisms. They often believe that Black students are mocking them whenever they code-switch between Black Vernacular expressions and Standard English language.

For example, Black students speak in Black Vernacular whenever they communicate with their peers. But, they will immediately switch to Standard English language in the presence of or when talking directly to teachers. Now, some students will arrogantly codify their speech in front of teachers once they become proficient at it. But, that's just the novelty effect arousing their youthful indiscretions. Teachers are often offended over their use of code-switching and arrogantly dismiss it as disruptive, which acts as a reason to send him to detention or the principal's office. For the most part, Black males believe it's not about them having or asserting a strong, dominant presence in the room. It's about teachers and their cultural expectations of Black male students.

For Blacks, what it means is most teachers look at Black males and assume they cannot cope in everyday school settings and are unwilling to engage the teacher in productive conversations. But, their beliefs create a process by which anticipation can lead the student to behave in ways that confirm teacher expectations. But, let me explain it to you in a way that I believe Dr. Joy DeGruy would. Her explanation for hostile attitudes given by teachers might sound something like what's stated in this next passage.

Teachers have a tendency to project their opposing intentions onto Black male students as a way to protect their self-esteem. First, they project onto students by justifying their attitude or behavior. Next, they relabel

Black students who they would like to further disadvantage. Relabeling is done in such a way that justifies them acting indifferent to the student. As a result, teachers often become manipulative and show no compassion toward him. Thus, anyone else who is uncomfortable around Black male students will feel totally vindicated when they are removed from school settings, a process we today call self-fulfilling prophecy. This self-fulfilling prophecy translates to a fear of social competition, which is, perhaps, the reason why so many Black males have trouble learning in school.

They also fail to understand why Whites believe their race will die out if national diversity continues to exist in America. Okay, they do understand that their birth population rate is, for whatever reason, at minus 0. But, statistics reveal that today's Whites are not having children as much as those from the baby boomer generation. Behavioralists purport that Whites are waiting until they're older to have children. Other Whites are making conscious decisions to not have children. Yet, many Whites strongly believe that their race is headed for genetic annihilation.

White people protest cultural adaptations like racial integration. Instead of simply withdrawing from mainstream society, they call for institutionalized segregation. Some even call for a race war. Hate groups like the Aryan Brotherhood, White Aryan Resistance (W.A.R.), and White Nationalists groups call for a civil war to end their problems.

In contrast, people are 99.99 percent the same in terms of their genetic disposition. Besides .005 percent of their genetic makeup being junk DNA, all humans are part of the same genetic species. For Blacks, White fear of diversity is clearly a problem that leads to a greater pathology surrounding the issue of race. In this way, the cultural attitude is surmised to be an inherent fear of crime. The result is Black males are beginning to reject all aspects of dominant society, including qualities where they appear to be acting White or feminine.

When Education Comes
At A Disadvantage

Second, the educational system is taught at a double standard. Referred to as Apartheid schools, these segregated schools grant privileges to Whites, most of whom are affluent. The goal of these schools is to keep different groups within the population separate, especially racial identity groups. Schools are kept divided by creating districts that the government divides into distinct geo-political or cultural sectors, districting cities and counties for all intended purposes. Black students more often attend separate schools from their White comparison counterparts. Many of their educators are young and often inexperienced. They're often ill-equipped to teach in low income areas.

Low income schools are like experimental labor-atories for the inexperienced. Regardless of race, and regardless of the precedence that should take place, more inexperienced teachers are given job opportunities in low income areas. The state board often says they hire those who are willing to work as if to say, no one experienced is willing to work with low income students. So, inner-city classrooms are often filled with new teachers who lack experience. Then there is the perpetually thorny problem of overcrowding in classrooms.

Many teachers are overburdened with oversized classrooms. These are the ones who lack the experience needed to help students succeed, not only in the classroom but in life. These young, inexperienced teachers are forced to teach in classrooms with 25 or more students per session. Many stay, knowing they cannot effectively teach in oversized classes. They will eventually gain the knowledge or technical skills needed to become proficient at teaching. But, it's more often at the expense or consideration of their students. Then you have new teachers who actually understand the cultural dynamics of teaching. They adapt pretty well in the classrooms. But, this book is not about them.

Schools in White districts usually have a class size of about 16-18 students. If these schools are affluent or historically White, class sizes can be smaller. When Whites and Blacks are forced to attend the same school, they're often divided into smaller groups that are kept apart. White students are placed in advance courses while Black students are kept in standard classes, or even remedial classes. Regardless of their academic abilities, White and Black students are kept apart. Either way, Black students are warehoused often knowing their teachers are ill-quipped to give them what's needed to compete, effectively, for job opportunities on the world market. For them, learning is a trial-and-error process, more error than trial, which leads us to our third and final reason why young Black males are refusing to learn.

Belief Of Their Social
Maladjustment

The third and final reason why Black males refuse to learn is the belief of their maladjusted attitude. Teachers believe that Black males are socially maladjusted and unable to cope in daily school settings or cope in teacher student relationships. Curiously, the average Black male is willing to learn but not from teachers who would prejudice their personal character by stereotyping students. Reverend Martin Luther King, Jr, DD, called the cultural attitude of young Black male students creative maladjustment. For King, the cultural attitudes of Black students were warranted and necessary.

Many are forced to deal with the unfairness of segregated schooling, a feeling of frustration that comes from trying to succeed in life while functioning at a disadvantage. If that's not bad enough, more are distressed at having been antagonized by the very people they're taught to admire, for example, people in authority. Police officers, teachers, school counselors, those who are supposed to protect and serve, teach, or give guidance, these role models consider Black males to be the enemy. White teachers are often condescending, behaving in ways that arrogantly dismiss Black students.

In this way, Black students refuse to learn from teachers or anyone who fails to show empathy for what they believe are cultural misunderstandings. Now, misunderstanding doesn't mean being socially maladjusted as readily assumed by most. Cultural misunderstandings happen when teachers arrogantly assume Black males are socially maladjusted and cannot learn. Then, they assume an air of indifference for Black students. Granted, Black students can be a bit sensitive, especially when race is involved.

In fact, many would love to set the record straight about US slavery. They believe that after 246 years of chattel slavery, 150 years of segregation, and prejudice and discrimination well into the new millennium, their psyche has suffered tremendous trauma. They say that they were never given an opportunity to heal, spiritually or emotionally, from the painful affliction caused by slavery, segregation, eugenics, et cetera. You name it and they, as a people, endured it! It's not like they had mental health professionals readily available to address their problems in their neighborhoods, either. Nor did their families understand they were modeling themselves after broken behavior. Why not? Well the fact is, part of that learned behavior is adaptive; because, it survived over the generations. So, dominant society calls it culture. Hence, their behavior becomes tolerable, ceteris paribus.

Further, Whites refuse to understand that Black suffering does not exist in the sense of direct contact but through social learning or modeling behavior. Part of the cultural attitude that continues to exist is based on the understanding that dominant society refuses to recognize or acknowledge Black suffering. Although today's Blacks are no longer subjected to harsh or cruel forms of abuse, remnants continue to exist in their environment. As a result, broken behavior continues to be learned by later generations who simply model themselves after significant others or loved ones. In this way, it often affects the way they think, feel, and behave toward strangers and others.

For example, a defensive posture given by many Black males when stared at too long is learned behavior. It develops from living in a hostile environment. Black students may justify this behavior by saying, in their neighborhood they do not stare directly at people too long. Why? Starring has negative connotations that make people feel uncomfortable. In this way, starring at the wrong person can cause conflict.

So, when a teacher stares too long at a Black student, the student considers that teacher to be a source of worry, stress, or trouble. In fact, the student will more likely challenge the teacher with a question: Who are you looking at? Or, why are you looking at me? If tensions escalate, that student might refuse to follow directions or fail to comply with school rules, especially if he perceives himself to be in an inappropriate situation, which could very well happen if the student feels like he is being manipulated or controlled.

Curiously, the behavioral exchange that takes place between the teacher and Black student is maladaptive. Both the teacher and student understand their actions are maladaptive. In fact, if the student believes that the teacher perceives his very presence to be threatening, he will consider it to be another reason why he should drop out of school. The first reason for dropping out is learning from your oppressors. The perception is the teacher doesn't like me. So then, why should I make an effort to show up and do work in this class? His attitude, a form of cultural nihilism, is the beginning process that leads students down the proverbial road to truancy, delinquency and, eventually, criminality.

Many of these students believe they are showing tolerance by attending class and giving teachers their time. They feel that they're wasting time in school trying to achieve an education. But a closer inspection of their attitude reveals a frustration that their aspirations will not come into fruition given the circumstances. In other words, Black students feel like they will never be hired for jobs that require using what they've learn in school just because of their racial identity. Besides, there are plenty White teachers in school who already confirm their fears of never being successful.

As well, Black students more often believe they will never become pillars of their communities. Hell, why would they want to when they are living in broken neighborhoods and rundown towns that once belonged to communities that no longer exist. They argue that these teachers who give motivational speeches about succeeding or being successful aren't from their neighborhoods or particular locality. In this way, they often need the teacher to show a little gratitude for their efforts in the relationship. It's often the lack of mutual respect that makes the relationship problematic. Neither considers the relationship symbiotic. Thus, there is always someone who views the other as a person who exploits the relationship without giving anything in return.

Many people feel that the teacher student interaction is a competition between competing egos arrogantly doing its best to dismiss the claims and demands of the other. But, this critical assessment is wrong. In fact, while there is a struggle with the ego, it's more often the teacher who clings to the notion of retaining his or her own importance or worth. That much is true! Young Black males, however, understand the nature of their argument and quickly frustrate. Why? Black children have no problem interpreting behavior and often become discouraged over the notion of having to endure someone who never wanted what was best for them. And, that creates esteem problems!

Proof comes in the form of trips to the principal's office, suspensions, expulsions, even school arrests. Interestingly, teachers say these incidences occur because of official school discipline policies. As a matter of fact, schools are suspending Black students too much, which sets them up for failure, delinquency and, eventually, juvenile detention. From that point onward, many of them develop a tendency to commit crimes.

School discipline policies were put in place to provide comfort and security for teachers, many ill-equipped to deal with children from low income areas.

Mandatory yearlong suspensions for any student found guilty of major school offenses adds to the problem of truancy, delinquency and, eventually, criminality. With many school districts adopting the Broken Window theory, students receive suspensions for minor infractions. The broken Windows theory is a criminological theory that states:

> Visible signs of crime, antisocial behavior, and civil disorder create an urban environment that encourages further crime and disorder, including serious crimes.

Thus, impudent replies to teachers, not attending class, or being otherwise disobedient or disruptive, translate into more suspensions for offenses previously unwarranted.

And with the educational system allowing school resource officers on campuses, Black male students are five times more likely to be arrested. Once arrested, they are taken to the juvenile court systems and criminalized for minor infractions. Juvenile records more often work to prevent many Black students, most of whom are misunderstood, from attending grade school. Without a proper education, having little to no vocational training, more of them socially maladjusted as well, which is a disposition that often forms from being raised in a hostile environment, many young Black males find themselves confronting more criminal charges in juvenile and criminal justice systems, a disturbing national trend called the school-to-prison pipeline.

I reported on the school-to-prison pipeline in a book entitled The Great Divide: The Social and Cultural Context of Inequality. It read:

> The school-to-prison pipeline took advantage of Black and poor families devastated by widespread illiteracy, mass unemployment, social neglect, economic abandonment, and intense police surveillance.

The school-to-prison pipeline (SPP) is based on the unfair and unequal treatment of young Black males who are incarcerated at disproportionate rates due to increasingly harsh grade school and municipal policies. It is such a disturbing trend, whereby young Black males, many of whom are misunderstood, are left to the streets of America to deal with illiteracy. What that means is more young Black males are abandoned by the school system, left vulnerable, with no skills to compete on the world market. This trend paved the way for Former President George Bush, Jr. to push his No Child Left Behind initiative. Its policies would soon be challenged.

No Child Left Behind

No Child Left Behind was a piece of legislation introduced into law in 2002. It was created for the purpose of holding schools accountable for how children learn and achieve. Unfortunately, it increased illiteracy for young Blacks. Many Black students were pushed through grade school without the benefit of actually learning. Most of the children who suffered were mainstreamed into classes above their academic abilities.

No Child Left Behind all but removed any chance of Black children successfully competing on the world market. Many of these children were socially maladjusted, others illiterate. Regardless of their academic abilities, under the No Child Left Behind Act, even children who were remedial would graduate regardless of their knowledge, especially whether or not they could read or write; hence, no child gets left behind.

Bush's efforts created a disturbing national trend wherein poor Black children would be funneled through the school-to-prison pipeline. No Child Left Behind would serve as a rule of conduct for K-12 public grade schools in America from 2002-2015.

Really, How Dumb Do You Think I Am is a chapter based on a collection of my personal thoughts and memories taken from Black people I've encountered over the years. Many, who I attended grade school with, refuse to receive an education so they can take their place in society as second-class citizens. For them, it's all or nothing. Unfortunately, they were more often left to endure illiteracy, poverty, and prison incarceration usually during adolescence. Some people call it willful ignorance, stating some people just refuse to learn. Again, Dr. King called it creative maladjustment.

My problem is not with the creative process itself. It is the naive lack of judgment associated with it. Black males from the younger generation find it easier to resist oppression with the benefit of their own experiences behind them. In hindsight, they will never gain the tactical advantage needed to achieve change. In this way, there needs be a continuation of education for Black people so they will not lose foresight of what will be necessary or may happen in the future.

What We Can Do To Resolve It

White teachers often assume Black male students are socially maladjusted since they refuse to learn. The condescending attitudes of teachers show Black students that they believe themselves to be intellectually superior. The lack of respect that takes place between the two is problematic. The problem is, while teachers deserve respect, it does seem that both teacher and student are responsible for developing and maintaining healthy intergroup relations. One view of how teachers should openly try to display better self-perceptions is to follow the understanding that all people, regardless of their cultural background, have the same intellectual processes and learning potential. However, there are cultural factors that determine how much knowledge one readily has and at what age.

The teacher-student relationship poses even greater problems for Black students. In many cases, there is an air of indifference between teacher and student. So for the student, the rule of law is to assume no White teacher has his best interest until they prove otherwise. But in the world of modernity, it will be beneficial to assume that teachers, regardless of race, are here to teach even though there is not much truth to otherwise support earlier conclusions. Their decision to learn, having other alternatives show a surprising amount of good judgment that accompanies maturity.

As always, we can appeal to the courts and our state representatives for changes in school curriculums, districting, et cetera. If that's not enough, then the next step is education reform. We can force change to the entire educational system or persuade the US President to do so. Apartheid school systems teach courses that abandon the truth about history. This style of education is harmful. Why? It is a coordinated attempt to hide unpleasant facts, especially in a political context. The problem is American children are abandoning education as a matter of principle. Their decision to leave without finishing it is based on the premise that young Black males are being miseducated.

To combat the problem of high dropout rates, perhaps, the most effective means of dealing with segregated school systems is to be vigilant about learning. Spending more time teaching our children to love education can have eventful outcomes for both younger and older people. To acquire the knowledge or skills on one's own initiative will strengthen what is needed or necessary to reach full equality.

The late great James Baldwin was a self-styled man. As a novelist, he explored the idea of change in America. Baldwin showed thoughtfulness as his writings made

Americans feel a gentle sadness about treating people differently through prejudice. His contributions to race, class, and gender in the United States offer us one example of how to fight against the tyranny of oppression.

In the next chapter, we will explore more on the intellectual processes of creative maladjustment. The question of whether or not integration was the trick behind the government's deceit awaits you in chapter 2.

Chapter 2
Behind The Government's Deceit

...I do not want to go to no suburbans not even Brooklyn. But Joyce wants to integrate. She says America has got two cultures, which should not be divided as they now is, so let's leave Harlem.

Langston Hughes (1994)

Lies, Tricks, And More Deceit

Blacks have been deceived by the United States of America. They pledge allegiance to the flag; and so they can be patriotic to the country. They're taught to model themselves after their nation's leaders, are expected to be proud supporters, and are told to be bold in defending its way of life. This, America decrees, is the will of God. But, America has yet to have a commemoration for the bravery of Blacks who fought to preserve it. The point is Blacks have a long history of serving this great nation. And what did it get them?

Fighting to defend America's honor started during the precolonial era, moving right along to the present day and age. So, you figure by now dominant society would accept Black people, regardless of their racial identity. Yet Blacks are still working to meet the cultural expectations of dominant society. Regardless of which roles they play, Black people are always met with White resistance. Postal carriers, government employees, business professionals, even spouses and homemakers are titles often met with resistance due to their racial identity.

Certainly, Blacks are welcome to serve in the military, to defend America's honor, and to die on the frontlines of a battle field. Serving is American. But for many Whites, the use of Blacks in the military threatens their way of life. Blacks are increasingly told there is no place in this country for them. Some Blacks are told by White civilians not wear the uniform in their home towns. Others are accosted for doing so. Centuries after chattel slavery, Whites continue to defend the notion that if Black people are taught patriotism, they will come to believe it is the duty of America to defend their rights.

Some people say that Blacks have been duped. Serving the government doesn't give them better access to resources or opportunities. They would have to become accepted members of American society before the government would open up opportunities for them to receive access. In order for Blacks to be accepted, they must be absorbed into society so that differences are minimized or eliminated; or, they become integrated into society under the same methods.

The problem is the government never intended to integrate Black people into the cultural mainstream. The concept of integration was only supposed to help them feel accepted. The trick was to end the Civil Rights movement without addressing the primary problems and concerns of Black folk. The primary concerns of Blacks were neither integration nor the establishment of civil rights. They wanted to address the maldistribution of resources that made segregation unjust or unfair. It was some time amid the second Civil Rights movement that Blacks lost focus on what they were fighting for. They originally wanted to correct the cultural legacies and burdens of American slavery. Later on, in 1967, the US Supreme Court ruled in favor of integration.

Integration was the lie behind the government's deceit. It was supposed to help Black people adapt to the mainstay of life. Thus, it was offered as a healthy adaptation of acculturation. The idea was to open communities to all citizens, regardless of race, ethnicity, religion, gender, or social class. Unfortunately, the concept of integration was never fully realized.

In 1967, the rest of White America began to retreat to the vanilla suburbs. The idea was to shutdown business industries, taking economic activities with them. In 1970, the United States government began to deindustrialize cities that were inherently Black. It limited the types of jobs and education Black people could consider. The government also took away resources needed to sustain Black communities. To further impact the sustainability of these communities, the government destroyed social structures that guaranteed Black sovereignty. So how does the government manage to keep Black people from reestablishing sovereignty in Black areas of America today? How is it that Black people never managed to rebuild their communities?

Well, that's simple! Mixed-income neighborhoods were introduced to Black people as a form of integration. Under integration, Blacks from various social classes and lifestyles would coexist in the same environment. The problem was they had nothing in common, which became apparent by the different levels of opportunity available to each social class. Thus, newly blended communities quickly decayed, especially from neglect.

To ensure integration would fail, banks began redlining. Bankers began to refuse loans, insurance, and other financial services to people and businesses in areas considered high financial risk. Heightening concerns for minor insurrections or civil unrest were just enough to justify refusing financial services to Black people.

In places like Baltimore, Maryland, the government removed proper funding from it after city residents rioted over the assassination of Reverend Martin Luther King, Jr. (1968). Banks would redline loans to Baltimore residents both directly by rejection and indirectly through selective pricing. Regardless of their financial status, and in spite of who could afford better, redlining forced many Blacks to permanently reside in mixed-income neighborhoods. Bankers also wanted to relocate city resources to newly developed suburban America. In this way, mixed-income neighborhoods would be further disadvantaged.

Years of neglect and decay left mixed-income neighborhoods crime-ridden. Those who could afford it, abandoned city neighborhoods to ensure their survival. Their goal was to protect their children from crime and violence. For those forced to stay, chronic life conditions imposed considerable stress on them and their children. Inadequate housing, dangerous neighborhoods, burdensome responsibilities, and economic uncertainties became potent stressors in their daily lives. These threatening and uncontrollable life events contributed to overwhelming feelings of powerlessness.

Then, in the mid 1980's, Black people gave up the chance to rebuild their communities. They surrendered their economy to Asians. Asians had the full financial support of their former countries. Thus, they were able to capitalize on Black store owners, many of whom were considered to be high financial risks. America's cities would soon reveal the intended purpose of ghettos.

For Asian Americans, businesses were booming. The Black economy became a part of the Asian job market. Minimarts, liquor stores, hair salons, and nail shops were dominated by Asian business professionals; and, they were doing well. Sadly, without a Black owned economy, Blacks would continue to be disadvantaged. Chocolate cities became rundown towns. Black neighborhoods were left broken from years of neglect and decay. City blocks were boarded up and abandoned by neighborhood residents. With the cluster of condemned houses spreading throughout entire cities, neighboring Black folk left, leaving these once thriving communities to become hoods or common shelter.

Thus, the question remains, why would any Black person choose to live in a society that continues to oppress them. With the government practicing deceit to disadvantage Black Americans, how are they supposed to receive quality assurance? In this way, young Blacks believe that learning from Whites is the last thing they need to do. Why? They feel that the government is setting them up for failure.

Today's Blacks have enough commonsense to understand that without a stable economy, to enter into a competitive struggle for wealth or power, is futile. They also understand that their education lacks serious value. Many employers feel a Black education has no substance. As a result, the business community believes Black people lack that strong sense of responsibility needed to compete effectively on the world market. In this way, selling yourself in a job interview will have no practical value or useful effect on a potential employer.

Their reasoning is quite simple: If you attain an education without having an economy, you will be forced to look for employment in other communities. In this regard, employers can place value on your education or extrinsic worth. Regardless of where you receive your education, it will never have the same value as your comparison counterparts who seek employment within their own communities. The idea of seeking employment in other communities is, in part, what White people call begging. The idea of begging is one of many reasons why young Black males refuse to model themselves after Whites.

Selling Yourself For A Job

Have you ever had career training? Career trainers prepare you to successfully negotiate job interviews and unique career opportunities. Even so, it's more likely you were asked to sell yourself to a potential employer. They want you to be polite, speak formal English, and submit yourself to an interviewer(s). In grade school, Black children are taught to model themselves after teachers, television and media personalities, and public figures. Modeling teaches students how to conduct themselves not only during future job interviews but in life.

Well, for young Black males, selling yourself has negative connotations. Many feel like the implication is suggestive of prostitution. The thought of them prostituting themselves for a job (i.e., for the love of money) is emasculating. In fact, they search for better ways of letting employers know of their desire to work.

"Exploiting your knowledge" takes on new connotations for Black males. It actually shows dominance over the topic during a job interview. When you exploit you knowledge, you're actually taking control of the interview. But, many career trainers push Black males to show a gentler, kinder personality during job interviews, hence the term "sell yourself." Although it may seem like I'm making more excuses for them, young Black males consider acting submissive to be the same as acting White. And for them, White men more often act feminine. The idea of young Black males functioning in life as effeminate is unappealing to them. Taking on negative connotations is another reason why they are refusing to adopt mainstream values. The idea is clear: If they are to pull themselves up by the bootstraps to make their own way in life, it should be done by their own admission, not by modeling after a people who oppressed them. But, therein lies the problem.

Modeling Behavior After
Those Who Oppressed You

Blacks are inherently American. They've been part of America's legacy since precolonial times. Like it or not, they are here to stay. Because their connection to slavery is considered forbidden, many experience feelings of alienation and identity loss. The loss causes them to feel a considerable amount of confusion and anxiety. Why? Essential features of their culture are lost and not replaced with those of the dominant society.

Today, many Blacks are troubled over having spent centuries modeling their behavior after a people who oppressed them. They tend to be unsupportive of anyone who chooses to assimilate their ideals to better dominant White society. They find the behavioral process problematic. Why so? It's more often brought on unconsciously as a particular way of behaving. They believe their behavior is triggered by external influences. These influences cause them to react to their situation because learned associations with acceptance are desirable. If true, then the problem with Black people is, regardless of how and where they assert themselves in society, they can only react to their oppression. Therefore, their behavior is involuntarily produced as a learned response.

There are Blacks who intentionally model their behavior after dominant society. People accuse them of adopting the social roles and behavioral expectations of their oppressors. Thus, many people consider them to be unconscious. And why is that? They are seemingly unaltered by or impervious to the damaging effects of oppression. They live their life concerned about their own interests, needs, and wishes while ignoring those of others. They are especially resistant to Blacks who upset the status quo. In terms of progression, evolution, or humanity, in terms of life itself, their mentality fails to make sense. Thus, you have to ask yourself why would an intelligent person who is repeatedly devaluated, degraded, and publicly humiliated, choose to adopt the values of their oppressors. What are the benefits?

For a select few, the benefits are better access to resources and opportunities. They are allowed to prosper in order to give Black people the illusion of conclusion. These Blacks are the byproducts of the White establishment, a group of elites who hold power and control American institutions. Now that we've cleared that up, one question remains: How can Black people function in ways that not only betray their people but their own principles? How can they be inspired by what's happening around them; are they inspired?

No, many Blacks are broken in spirit by the overwhelming stress of oppression. They internalize their fears because of a real or imagined pressure to conform. They also accept that they cannot function productively in society without modeling after the ways of dominant Whites. Although they may not approve of or agree with it, they discriminate against their own people to protect their self-interests. Still, their social class and status advance continuously because of the lies hidden behind the government's deceit.

Modeling After Broken Behavior

Modeling oneself after loved ones and significant others can also be problematic. In Black areas of society, it has a dark history. In many cases, and through no fault of their own, Blacks model themselves after broken behavior. This brokenness is passed down from previous generations without people taking notice. Why? Part of the behavior is adaptive. We know this to be true since researchers found evidence of adaptive behavior through the Black family lineage. They also find that broken behavior is something not readily questioned or challenged. Why? The behavior is mistaken for Black culture. That means it results from shared beliefs and practices readily identified during a particular place or time to which their ancestors felt it requisite for a healthy society. The types of disciplines that existed and continue to exist in Black areas of society are classic examples.

Have you ever heard of the old adage spare the rod, spoil the child? It is a variation of a passage written in proverbs 13: 24 of the King James Version Christian Bible. Its meaning has many interpretations, some taken literal. For example, Black parents tend to beat their children when they are disciplinary problems. Beatings are the literal interpretation of the passage.

Beatings serve as a corrective measure to prevent delinquent behavior. In many cases, parents who are discipliners find beatings necessary to prevent their children from developing criminal behavior. So, they often quote the passage to justify their methods even though it is considered child abuse by today's standards.

Beatings have a long history in Black society. It was adopted from chattel slavery. Slavery masters used it as a corrective measure to prevent enslaved Africans from being disobedient and often, from running away. In 1851, Samuel A. Cartwright hypothesized that slaves often thought of running away due to a mental disorder called drapetomania. The treatment he prescribed in the prevention of Africans fleeing captivity was frequent whippings.

Another form of broken behavior is denigrating your children even when they are exceptionally good. For example, there are two mothers visiting their children's elementary school, one Black and the other White. Two of their children are exceptional students and are doing well in their studies. The Black mother turns to the White mother and says, Geezes, you child is truly gifted." The White mother is gleaming with pride and joy because of the compliments she just received from the Black mother. She brags and rightfully so. Later, the White mother learns that the child of the Black mother is out excelling her child. She, in kindness, returns the compliment to the Black mother who immediately begins to denigrate her own child, bringing up her faults as if to say the child is problematic.

Now, let's give it context! Think about how Black children were sold during slavery. As property, Black women had no right to their children. So when a child who was thought to be old enough to perform the duties of adult slaves, he or she would be sold off the plantation to work. Remember, sometimes being sold meant working the fields. At other times, it meant bearing children to be sold off as commodity in the slave industry.

The best way to wage an argument with the slave master was to convince him that her child was incompetent. She often denigrated her children to protect them from the ravishing ways of the slave master. For example, the mother would misinform her master by telling him that her child was dumb and could not produce quality children. Thus, the Black woman had to be persuasive when arguing the protection of her children.

It is not only possible but common for the greatest ancestors of Black people to have endured or undergone some form of psychological trauma as a consequence of slavery. Its impact often had immediate and strong effects on their perceptions. From the point of infliction, the way their mental faculties processed information about their surrounding environment or immediate situation was more often the results of broken behavior. Entire communities were built on these broken perceptions. Now, let's fast forward four hundred years later.

Black women have been left to endure trauma without the aid of mental healthcare or national recovery assistance to lessen the impact of systemic oppression. In this case, the Black mother doesn't denigrate her children as an act of disrespect. It is more likely an unconscious fear that, in some way, her White counterpart, be it man or woman, has the power to break up the Black family unit. The Black mother's attitude toward her is an example of modeling broken behavior.

The fact that, as a parent, the mother continues to denigrate her children in front of her White counterpart is testament to the trauma that continues to impact Black people today. Yet, people continue to think of it as customary, tradition, or culture for Black folk. But, it's not! It's a greater problem surrounding the issue race. Thus, what White society calls Black culture today is more often a psychopathology that needs to be addressed.

Today, Blacks use variations of Cartwright's system of abuse to include actual beatings, paddling, spankings, et cetera. Other, softer variations of disciplining include washing a child's mouth out with soap, standing children in the corner as a method of timeout, and more. The problem is these disciplinary methods are maladaptive. Even use of the word discipline is a cover that masks the negative effects of abuse, thus it's maladaptive. One of my favorite commercials used a slogan to campaign against child abuse in the early 1980's. The slogan was as stated: Abused children grow up to be child abusers. The ad conveyed a message so powerful, the commercial industry removed it from television.

It has long since been proven that children who are abused during childhood will develop into child abusers later in life. It is estimated that nearly 700,000 children are abused in the United States each year. Most of these children, an estimated 678,000, were victims of unique incidents as reported in 2018 by the National Children's Alliance. James Baldwin spoke to the effectiveness of William Shakespeare's genius insight on the notion of correcting or fixing broken behavior. Baldwin writes:

> The greatest poet in the English language found his poetry where poetry is found: in the lives of the people. He could have done this only through love— by knowing… that whatever was happening to anyone was happening to him.

Baldwin found solace in knowing Shakespeare shared his burden, which renewed his hopes in the humanity of others. Thus, Baldwin's literary critique of Shakespeare was a revelation that revealed his own truth. That while he spent most of his life feeling like a sad or regrettable thing, he knew that White people were suffering much in the same way he suffered. In that moment, Baldwin knew he had a divine truth to raise the will of humanity.

In the same sense, Blacks are an exceptional people. They are the only people in the world who were and still are forced to better their lives without the assistance or influence of other people. In fact, they were never given an opportunity to heal. Nor did they ever receive mental health support, economic recovery assistance, or federal relief aid to end their suffering. Yet today, Blacks are tasked with having the responsibility to heal the rift that caused their people to hemorrhage spiritually or emotionally.

Many mental health disorders developed from the system of slavery. Not only did it affect the psychology of White people, it traumatized Blacks, many of whom continue to suffer its ill-effects. Today, quite a few disorders remain unverified or untested, especially for genetic and hereditary traits.

Modeling Behavior After
A History of Lies

Yet, another reason why Black males are so resistant to learning is the inaccurate or misleading way their government reports on its history. This statement is true not only for Blacks studying American history, Early British literature, or Western philosophy, but those who learn their family history through oral or written tradition.

First, the problem with American history is it's a tale about Whites and their struggles, victories, and triumphs. It's also taught in a way that arrogantly dismisses the roles of Black people: their achievements, acclaims, and contributions. History can give people the fundamentals needed to effect change in the world. But with America constantly whitewashing history, Black males find much of the information contradictory.

Some people find historical accounts of American history contradictory. There is a contradiction between how it relates to their past experiences and present actualities. Having to learn someone else's history, especially when it's a testament to your suffering, puts you at a great disadvantage. This type of learning is called controlling the narrative. It is how dominant society awards an advantage to the very people who oppressed you and your people.

Right now, at this very moment, you should understand why so many Black children choose to not-learn history. Still, if it's not clear to you, then think of it in this way. What does American history have to do with the price of tea in China? This statement is actually a philosophical question. The point is, if you can answer this question, you make a connection with history in a way that should be shared with everyone. And yes, I've answered that question before.

Young Blacks understand how whitewashing history puts them at an unfair disadvantage. For example, US historians often romanticize the history of worlds and the wars fought that shaped these great nations into legends. The United States and Great Britain claim the world's greatest battles and the world believes them. Their claim is another way of controlling the narrative. But, when you attempt to hide unpleasant facts, especially in a historical context, you initiate problems and create complications that eventually run out of control. For example, we know now that American historians gave inaccurate reports of history in ways that misled its citizens well into the new millennium. Many Black historians criticized the 2019 American biographical historical film Harriet. They weighed in on its inaccuracies, sighting fictitious accounts of characters that depicted Black males as the main problem source and the engine behind slavery.

In creation of these movie characters, it also revealed subliminal messages to include a supposed envy of the White man's possession of a penis. There were also role reversals whereby slavery was depicted as a misunderstood practice gone wrong, eating away at slave masters as it could not be controlled. Frankenstein's monster, slavery was depicted as a thing that harmed or destroyed what was necessary for a productive society.

Movie characters like "Bigger Long," whose name has obvious connotations, symbolized a supposed theme of progression Whites find troubling among young Black males today. Harriet's character represented a disturbing trend in behavior that characterized the struggles of America's pride movement.

My point is that the Hollywood version is far removed from the truth. Its inaccuracies are the reasons why so many Black males will not-learn from White people. Certainly, family accounts of her story tell a different tale. They give vivid accounts of Harriet's harrowing actions as past down from both oral and written traditions. Truth of the matter is Harriet's story is quite different. Although Hollywood claims the film was well intended, skeptics believe its inaccuracies were meant to distort Harriet Tubman's rightful place in history.

Some people remain skeptical that the government will always lie about its past, the current state of affairs, and its future endeavors. Others believe it's only a matter of time before government officials tell the truth. A few public intellectuals agree that a country built on lies will crush under the impact of its own weight if it airs forbidden secrets. They say that distortions in America's history serve to teach the world of absurdities to mask the vicious lies behind its tricks and deceit.

What We Can Do To Resolve It

In order to end the lies and tricks behind the government's deceit, we must dispel inaccurate or misleading accounts of America's history. But, there lies a trick behind that trade.

There are two approaches we can use to resolve this problem. The first approach is incremental and designed to prevent faulty education. It involves a grassroots approach to education reform. The goal here is to change and improve educational policies by correcting faults, removing inconsistencies and abuses, and imposing modern methods or values on the US Department of Education.

We have to persuade or force the US President to adopt more acceptable educational methods and curriculums as a profession. Here, the idea is to get the US President to execute educational policies for the nation that reflect its true heritage. Or else, we push for reorganization and improvement. Why? The curriculum for the entire educational system contains flaws, especially ones that hide unpleasant facts about history. The argument is academic courses have historical components that give inaccurate accounts of history, especially in a political context. Thus, there needs to be reforms designed to prevent faulty education, especially in the social or political sphere.

The second approach is to reject conventional society and live in an alternative way. In order to do so, we must reestablish a separate and distinct cultural system. I use the word reestablish because there was once a thriving system of Black communities in America. Black communities cannot be revived without reestablishing its own economy, a code of conduct, and political independence.

Blacks must first agree to actively and consciously pursue economic interests, together, in order to create a sustainable and stable economy for themselves. Shared beliefs and practices help to form a particular set of values we characterize as culture. And, a culture is requisite for a healthy society. The idea is to create an independent economy, which will give Black people the ability or right to reestablish their own communities in order to effect change in their intellectual progression.

Black communities cannot exist without rebuilding their own social structures and community resources. They must become remarkable in their resilience and adapt in a society that continues to tell them what's best. Community support systems, such as churches, recreational and community associations, family associations, and educational institutions must reflect the persistence of Black culture. A financial system, such as banks, insurance companies, and stock exchanges, businesses that permit the exchange of money, must also reflect the persistence and presence of Black culture.

Last, Blacks will have to master the art of negotiation. They need to develop impressive strategies for adapting to life in America. They must also be ready to negotiate with world cultures. Their presence on the world market will have a powerful impact in how dominant society interacts with them. Essentially, the lack of interaction threatens the fundamental basis of equality for Black people today.

In this chapter, we have discussed many facets of techniques that the government uses to deceive Black people, including some ideas about how they should be treated and the true nature of government. In the next chapter, we will turn our attention exclusively to problems Black people have with using an ascribed identity.

Chapter 3
The Problem With Having An Ascribed Identity

Until the color of your skin is the target, you will never understand.

Angela Davis (1944 - Present).

There is no problem with having an ascribed identity unless you are a member of the oppressed. People use it to categorize or label individuals and groups according to an oversimplified and habitual way of thinking about them, especially with reference to certain social stigmas it produces. In this regard, an *ascribed identity* is a name or label usually assigned to people at birth and recognized as belonging uniquely to that person or group.

Black Americans—perhaps the most oppressed racial group on earth—were assigned their identity by dominant White society. Originally, Black Americans were largely from West Africa. As part of their indoctrination into chattel slavery, they had every aspect of their African identity removed. They were baptized in the name of Christianity, and then assigned European names like Toby, Jane, and William. Why? Slave owners believed it would help them conform to cultural expectations.

The methods used to control enslaved Africans were simple yet diabolical. For the slave owner, free thinking was a matter of will as much as opportunity. Given the right opportunity, a willful African could trigger a slave rebellion. Therefore, they had to be thoroughly and systematically broken to discourage them from independent thinking or accepting other opinions. They were deprived of their culture and heritage. They were not allowed to practice their religion nor allowed to wear articles of clothing that could signify independence. The idea was to keep them physically strong but psychologically weak and dependent on the slave owner.

Fast forward to the new millennium and Blacks from the younger generation are rejecting any names or labels assigned to them by dominant society. Labeling is more often based on cultural stereotypes. Stereotypes justify the continued display of negativity directed at Blacks. Labeling Black people helps White people to remove any feelings of discomfort they may develop from behaving cruelly or unjustly toward Blacks, especially after neglecting their spiritual or emotional wellness. In this regard, Whites often demonized and demoralized Black people as quarrelsome, criminal, or disrepute. Neglect, abuse, and state sanctioned violence are often the results of White people assigning negative labels to Black people. In this way, labels falsely justify the maltreatment of Black people.

Often, it's the malicious intent of being labeled that causes Blacks to reject their ascribed identities. In this way, dominant society uses labels to remove the humanity from people they are about to victimize. Why? Labeling reduces the potential victim to the status of a simple object. It then becomes easy for them to remove any feelings of regret that might occur at the mere thought of victimizing another human. In other words, the less humane your victims appear, the easier it becomes to victimize them without experiencing shame and doubt.

For example, Black people continue to die from official murders, largely because the police learned to justify their violence. What that means is police aren't afraid of being penalized because they learned to work within the letter of the law. They use technical terms like perpetrator, criminal intent, and lawless to justify using obsessive force against them. From that point onward, Blacks are no longer viewed as human. In this way, White police officers feel totally vindicated when state-sanctioned violence ends in the official murder of Black people.

The overwhelming feeling of satisfaction police get when Blacks die in their custody increases the consistency or compatibility between their actions or beliefs. After all, Blacks are marginal; and the term marginal means that Blacks, for whatever reason, are so maladjusted they will never adapt to the mainstay of life. It seems that their maladjustment makes it okay for the police to display an overwhelming amount of aggression. Thus, "the faces of victimization can change daily, but the abuse will remain the same."

Although we've only read a few paragraphs thus far, it should be easier to imagine the negativity associated with being labeled. Labeling can pigeonhole people into difficult or unpleasant circumstances from which there is no clear or easy way out. Labeling causes people to categorize and judge others unfairly. We often assign labels to people without giving it a great deal of thought. The harm associated with labeling is real even if the intent is not. The result is the tendency to dismiss people as unimportant.

Race is an ascribed identity. It is used to divide the world's population into groups of humans based on physical characteristics like skin tone or color. White, Black, Brown, Red, and Yellow are color schemes we use to categorize or label humans. Race has been argued to be either a social construct or a biological construct. The US Supreme Court recognizes race as a biological construct. Its members stated that any person having 1-16th Black ancestry in their linage will not be considered White in accordance to the principles so written in law. The law poses considerable problems for people, especially those who have dual heritages.

Biracials tend to reject the subordinate half of their dual heritage. They consider it to be a heavy burden that weighs on their very existence. As a result, many of them abandon their moral obligations to uplift their own race. For example, newly elected Vice President Kamala Harris identified with her mother's race. As a result, she distanced herself from people who were of her father's race. It appeared that her father (a Black man) caused considerable problems for Kamala.

As District Attorney (DA) in the state of California and as US States Attorney, Kamala had a notorious reputation for issuing draconian punishments to Black men. It was as if each conviction was a symbolic attack on her father. The harsher the sentencing, the more distance she put between herself and Black men. Today, arguably, she identifies with her father's race when it's convenient.

The Problem With Having
An Ascribed Status

Terms like marginality and minority remove complexity from people even though, as a racial group, they may be quite complex and multifaceted. Thus, each one can be more complicated than simple labels. In fact, these terms are a part of an ascribed (social) status usually assigned to Black people at birth or assumed, involuntarily, later in life. In this way, an ascribed status lets people know your relative position in society, social standing in a cultural group, or marks your place in the world. The problem with having an ascribed status or identity, for that matter, is that it's neither earned nor chosen but assigned. Thus, by definition, and for the purpose of this book, an *ascribed status* is the social position usually assigned to a Black person at birth.

Dominant society assigned the status marginal to Black people. Why? The essential features of their cultures are lost and not replaced by those of the larger, more dominant society. Although the status appears to be justified, the assignment is based on a negative stereotype. Marginalization is usually associated with confusion and identity loss. Thus, people more often assume that marginal groups have no culture. Quite the contrary, it doesn't mean that a marginal group has no culture. It simply means that as a group, they may be disorganized and unsupportive of individuals who are willing to relinquish their cultural identity so they can adjust and move into the larger society.

An ascribed status remains constant throughout a person's life and is therefore inseparable from the positive or negative stereotypes we link to one's ascribed identity. For example, people of African origin are assigned the ascribed identity Black. Since America is controlled and regulated by Western government, Blacks are assigned the ascribed status minority. Regardless of their successes or failures, they will forever be assigned the ascribed status minority. This realization is true of any minority with the exception of those who can cloak their identity in racial secrecy. The idea of assigning such statuses exists across cultures, within all societies, and is based on race, culture, ethnicity, nationality, gender, and ancestry.

In another example, the people of Panama were considered one race. Later, after continuous contact with Western government, they began ranking themselves into categories of either White or Black. For years, their social status was based on their level of productivity. And they were socially classified in that way. Unfortunately, under the influence of Western culture, their social categories began to take on different connotations. Their new system of classifying was based on color. Light-skinned Panamanians were grouped into categories as White. Dark-skinned Panamanians were grouped into categories as Black. Black Panamanians inherited the city much like Blacks in the United States. Then the Panamanian government redistributed much of the nation's wealth, giving an added advantage to White Panamanians who were benefitting from their newfound status.

Today, White and Black Panamanians are pitted against one another. There is very little unity among their people. And a once modest nation is now heavily influenced by Western culture. In this way, ascribed statuses are stratified by social, economical, and political systems that give advantages to or take advantages away from people based on family origins or families with more or less resources than others. It is also important to point out that ascribed statuses are most notably found in social caste systems where there is a ridged social hierarchy set in place with low social mobility.

Certainly, there is no way to stress the negative effect of stereotypes that are assigned to Black people. Again, we're talking about social statuses that follow people throughout the lifespan. For example, many Africans resent being labeled Black in America. They view labeling as wrong or unjust. They understand that labeling has negative connotations that make people dislike Blacks. As a result, Africans socially distance themselves from Black Americans.

In many cases, Africans learn to discriminate against Black Americans. They discriminate for the same reasons Whites do. Why? Africans blame Black Americans for the negativity directed at them. Many Africans believe Black Americans provoked Whites into enslaving them. Their continued negativity is believed to be a direct result of Black mediocrity. Thus, many Africans are more than willing to exploit Black Americans to gain acceptance from dominant society.

To be typecast as Black in America means never having the opportunity to be equal. As a result, many Black immigrants feel like social outcastes. They understand that no matter what they contribute to American society, they will forever be saddled with social stigmas. Their tendency to begrudge Black Americans comes from the fear of being grouped into the same social categories as them. Thus, they discriminate against Black Americans to gain White peer approval. Noted: Many Blacks across the African diaspora share the same sentiments as those who immigrate to the United States. Perhaps, it's a part of becoming westernized, that is, to adopt the beliefs of their North American counterparts.

Now, I do understand that my statements are awkward; that not every Black American shares my sentiments. Most do not! Nor is it my way of saying all Africans feel this way about Black Americans. Many do not! But, my sentiments are real. These are, of course, my personal experiences interacting with Africans or Blacks across the African diaspora.

I do not wish to end this chapter on a note of cheap sentiment. So, I will continue on with a further discussion of why ascribed statuses are problematic to Black Americans.

Pitted Against One Another

If you cannot tell by now, ascribed statuses pit people against one another. As characteristic of caste systems, ascribed statuses are set up to cause opposition between people. Opposition is created to cause division among cultural groups. The recent appointment of Presidential nominee Joe Biden as the 46 elected President of the United States sent America into strong opposition. President Donald Trump opposed President-elect Joe Biden's appointment to the Oval Office. And on January 6, 2021, many of Trump's supporters took to the Nation's Capitol to stage a coup in his defense.

Trump supporters coordinated a sudden and violent attempt to overthrow the Nation's Capitol. They wanted to show their disapproval of Trump from being removed from the Oval Office. They attempted to seize political power, especially to regain control of Black Americans, many of whom were told they would be reenslaved if the coup attempt proved to be successful.

Americans witnessed appalling acts of cowardice and treason, not just among those who attempted the coup, but political party-members as conspirators. Many watched with pride, the unexpected and dangerous attempt to overthrow the Nation's Capitol. President Trump was said to have been watching the coup attempt from the White House bedroom. Apparently, he was upset only about how unacculturated his supporters looked as they seized the Nation's Capitol. Democratic members of Congress once again called for the immediate impeachment of the Commander-in-Chief. Oddly, there was no failsafe in place to prevent a sitting President from staging a coup attempt.

The acting Attorney General downplayed the threat and danger to the nation. Afterwards, President Trump and Republican Party members quickly began taking steps to try and pardon his supporters for participating in the coup attempt. Meanwhile, the Nation fell into a state of internal discord, strife, and confusion. There was division among Republicans in America. Conservatives were pitted against one another, for example. Democrats reprioritized their political agenda, focusing their efforts on legalizing 11 million immigrants. The generation gap increased, widening the cultural divide. And as for minorities who were torn by divided loyalties, well, they remained hopeful.

Black Americans remained divided over their voting priorities. It appeared that many did not get the memorandum that Joe Biden was a liberal racist as he excluded Black Americans from his political agenda. Biden and Harris both agreed that Black-themed issues were low in priority.

Several days earlier, President-elect Joe Biden held a private meeting at the White House with Black community leaders and political representatives. He discussed his plans to restore America to normalcy. In his speech, he reprioritized his political agenda, further moving Black Americans to a permanent underclass. If they are neglected, Black Americans will become so under-privileged that they may never regain the footing needed to move into the cultural mainstream. And with Kamala Harris as Vice President-elect, was there ever any wonder why Blacks from the younger generation were refusing to vote?

The System Works!

Regardless of what people think, the system does work. The question is who does it work for? American society functions as an Apartheid or social (caste) system. It separates various demographics into distinct cultural systems and gives White people privileges others do not receive. Although rights and advantages are more often enjoyed by the cultural elite, Whites generally benefit from this system of privilege. The result is Blacks are more often socially excluded and persecuted.

Scholars once thought White people did not understand how they benefited from a system of privilege. For years, many Whites hid behind a culture of victimhood whereby they convinced the public that White people feared for their personal safety. Many people believed personal safety was the reason behind the government stratifying the social system. In this way, any attempts to change the system were considered to be hostile. Activists appealed to the public for years, trying to convince dominant society of the need for change. They even began to receive assistance from White scholars.

White scholars played a small but increasing role in educating the public on the need for change. Their job was to educate or inform White Americans that White privilege was the real threat. They informed them about America's founding fathers and their quest to rule as kings over humanity. They ensured them that their conquest was about controlling and manipulating the outcome of humanity or, at least, to ascribe contentment to those who were the most humane.

Today, it is more than obvious that America is founded on a system of White privilege. Those who subscribe to this system are part of a ridged social hierarchy that control oppressed sects of society. The problem is that in order for Whites to benefit from it, they have to put other people at a disadvantage. This problem is where it all begins.

America's social system was founded on White privilege. It is no coincidence that the US presidency has only been occupied by people who share the same genetic inheritance. Black people are kept at a disadvantage in this way. What makes matters worse is dominant society takes selfish or unfair advantage of their privileged situation, usually for personal gain. In fact, America's social system is setup to keep Black people in a no win situation. Allow me to explain.

The system is stratified by social, economical, and political systems. These systems divide people into five main classes. Each class is categorized according to importance. This ranking creates White privilege whereby a ridged social hierarchy is put into place to benefit and give advantages to a relatively small group of people, usually as a result of wealth or social status. These advantages, rights, and, in most cases, benefits are not readily shared with Black people.

Truth of the matter is wealth is supposed to gradually benefit the poorest as a result of its increase among the richest. But in reality, poor people, especially Black people, remain disadvantaged. Although this type of discrimination has been illegal for quite some time, Black people continue to find themselves disadvantaged in most areas of American government and in today's society.

Older Blacks talk about voting so that the system of White privilege becomes available to everyone. They say this is what Foundational Black Americans died trying to overcome. "Vote for yourself if you have to; but vote," some say! But the question young Blacks have is why vote when their vote only count toward the popular vote. In this way, Black people need to be as strategic about voting as their foundational elders were during the Civil Rights movement.

Between the Electoral College and the popular vote, young Black males aren't as concerned about voting today. Many believe that if our foundational elders were alive to revisit their struggles, they would change their voting priorities. That is to say, many of the young believe our foundational elders would completely change their priorities. Or maybe they would opt to promote a new political agenda. Dr. Martin Luther King, Jr. wanted to reprioritize Black Americans. He wanted to refocus their agenda on economic and political independence.

In the end, King decided that wealth creation was an equitable means to achieving equality for Blacks in America. Dr. King was assassinated in April of 1968 after he publicly announced the Poor People's Campaign. After his assassination, the Southern Christian Leadership

Conference (SCLC) decided to continue campaigning under the leadership of Ralph Abernathy, its newest president. On Mother's Day, May 12, 1968, led by Coretta Scott King, thousands of women from every walk of life descended on Washington, D.C., as the first surge of protest demonstrators.

Ethel Kennedy was among the many women who attended the Mother's Day opening of Resurrection City. Resurrection City was a National Park (Parkland) used as a temporary settlement for protest demonstrators. The Department of Interior closed down Resurrection City on June 24, 1968, after the permit to occupy it expired. Needless to say, today's young Blacks are more concerned about political and economical independence. The older generation continues to be preoccupied with racial integration.

There is a great miscarriage of justice and it involves the exploitation, oppression, and humiliation of Black Americans. Many Whites subscribe to a system that disadvantages Black people. However, young Blacks refuse to take part in a system that continues to disadvantage them. Older Blacks feel like the younger generation is denying themselves of unique opportunities to advance.

Young Blacks understand that many of the scientific breakthroughs that modernized America were made by Black Americans. Yet today, dominant Whites continue to believe that Black people are a social liability. They say Blacks simply cannot compete in a modern society. Curiously, Black women received more PhD's in the new millennium than any other gender identity group in the United States. They are the best educated and fastest growing group in America. Yet, the belief of social dominance is true for the larger majority of today's Whites. In fact, the real threat to White people or White privilege is the notion of sharing political control with Black people.

In a recent turn of events, White people revealed a deep pathology surrounding the issue of race. Most recently, a series of events led to an attempt to overthrow the US Government. It revealed that White people have an exaggerated sense of superiority, usually as a result of wealth or their ascribed status. Many Trump supporters believe that America belongs to them and their people. In fact, they were agitated over the notion of cultural diversity.

Some Whites believe that cultural diversity would lead to the genetic annihilation of the White race. At least, it appeared to be the catalyst that accelerated their aggression. Sad to say, more Whites believed they had a right to dominate and rule over others who were weaker than them. They wanted to push Black people into involuntary servitude.

The notion of social dominance dates back to the age of Cro-Magnon when the earliest known form of Europeans wiped out Neanderthals in their quest for supremacy. Even after the medieval period, the urge to conquer others was reinforced by the Moorish conquest to civilize the people of Europe. Slavery, eugenics, and discrimination were all European attempts to exert dominance over others. However, the problem was only a small group of White people truly benefited from it. In this way, people have become alert and vigilant about social dominance or the system of White supremacy.

The idea that dominant Whites have the ability to segregate people from the cultural mainstream or divide them into smaller, subordinate groups, each with a different set of priorities, which alone causes division among the American people. Racial division is perhaps the main problem with having an ascribed status. Thus, there is continued work to be done. Now that America has reared its ugly, xenophobic head, what's the next step for Americans? How do we work toward building greater change? Do we separate and work toward building our own? Or, do we work on racial integration with the rest of society, a concept that has never been fully realized?

What We Can Do To Resolve It

What we can do to resolve this problem is continue to educate or inform people. Communication continues to play an essential role in determining the nature, shape, or structure of American culture. I sense that our belief in humanity will guide us through the entire process.

First, we need to recognize or acknowledge that double standards exist well within the long-established customs and traditions of American culture. And these double standards are viewed as a set of precedents. In order for Blacks to receive equal treatment under the law, especially when those bodies of law are inadequate in the attainment of justice, they must put into practice a new set of priorities. These priorities should give instruction on how to instigate social change.

Second, we need to focus our attention on social justice. As we read in our discussion on problems with ascribed identities, Black Americans are of a social class so underprivileged that they are at-risk of becoming a permanent underclass. They continue to struggle for fairness and better opportunities under the constant threat of poverty and racism. Hence, it is important for society to turn its attention to the ways politicians treat Black Americans.

The way in which they are treated should be the same or comparable to any supporting members of the two major political parties in the United States. In this way, the same political policies that apply to Whites should apply to Blacks. Any concerns or grievances about political representation should be treated in the utmost regard as applied by the principles of ethics and fair play so written in law.

And third, there should be a failsafe in place to ensure the safety of democracy. It will prevent sitting presidents and politicians of the United States from overthrowing the government and seizing political power. It should be designed to exchange power in the event of a fault or failure in politics. As it stands now, the Electoral College functions as a failsafe to ensure the cultural elite remain in power. It puts the American public under the impression that their vote matters when, in fact, it's the members of the Electoral College who make the final decision. The vote should be left in the hands of American citizens. Thus, as a matter of principle, the Electoral College should be abolished.

Another way to create a failsafe is to rewrite The Constitution. It should be rewritten or its amendments ratified in order to correct, update, improve, or adapt a new set of priorities. Revisions should take precedence over the seven articles and 27 amendments previously adopted. And, it should ensure the freedoms, rights, and responsibilities of Blacks to live peaceably. Contrary to the rhetoric written in the Constitution (1789), the Union established justice and secured the blessings of freedom for the cultural elite and their future generations. Remember, it is no coincidence that all presidents except for Donald Trump are blood relatives. Nor is it coincidental that the founding fathers belonged to a secret society of men who were united for a common purpose shared by that same organization today. A political failsafe will put more power into the hands of citizens to ensure America stays a free nation.

Advocates press for greater inclusion of Blacks to liberate them from traditional socially imposed constraints like those arising from stereotyping. They hope that the establishment in Washington, DC will give increased attention to Black people and treat their problems with more respect and greater dignity.

In this chapter and others, we have seen that ascribed identities like names, labels, and terms are social constraints. These constraints provide contexts for the way in which Black people are perceived. In addition, ascribed statuses like marginality and minority are designed to remove the complexity from an individual and group even though some are quite complex and multifaceted. We now understand how or why having an ascribed identity can be problematic. In this next chapter, we will have a discussion on Black people and their search for an avowed identity.

Chapter 4
The Search For An Avowed Identity

I am not afraid of my truth anymore and I will not omit pieces of me to make you comfortable.

(Anonymous, 2021).

The Vow To Develop
A New Identity

Black people are vowing to develop a new identity. It's part of an effort to break from western influence, to become a separate and distinct cultural system. It can be affirming, their commitment to the development of an identity they feel is right or true for them. Developing an avowed identity can be as simple as creating unique names for you and your children. Or, it can be as grand as identifying with or connecting to significant yet forbidden figures in your past to better show the world who paved the way for your success. Often, but not always, it involves exploring or learning your heritage. But for Black Americans, it definitely involves learning their heritage. It especially involves learning their immediate heritage.

There is a reason why Black Americans are choosing to learn their immediate heritage. They lost both cultural and psychological contact with Africa. The need to belong has yet to be replaced with essential features of those in the Western world. So for many, it's no longer about finding acceptance from either nation. Their commitment to Western culture and intrigue with Africa no longer appeals to them. Black Americans do believe that they should bear names that reflect their racial origin as well as geopolitical heritage. After all, they would love to help preserve their rich history. It is a large part of who they are. In fact, they understand that without having some knowledge of African and American history, there would be no need to establish a new identity. And for that reason, many are grateful.

However, neither nation has done anything in the way of connecting with Black Americans. When Africans come to America, many feel like they must compete with Black Americans. They model themselves after dominant Whites, most of whom believe that the presence of Black Americans threaten their fundamental existence. It's the fear of social competition that causes a rift in relations between these distinctly different cultural systems.

At one point in time, the need to belong would have resulted in a considerable amount of confusion and anxiety. But today's Blacks simply choose to search for their own identity, one uniquely attuned to them. In developing their own identities, they correct personal, social, or cultural indignities that Western culture imposed on them throughout their intellectual history.

Unfortunately, when the Western world character-izes someone who is Black, it's often based on cultural stereotypes. Typically, Black people say they cannot effectively compete in the world using an identity based on cultural stereotypes. The world understands that Black progress is modeled behind White success. In fact, the world uses Blacks as a marker of success. If immigrants want to know how well they are doing in Western society, they compare their success to that of Blacks. If immigrants find they're doing better than them, then they know they're being treated fairly. In fact, most immigrants understand that if they are to succeed in Western society, they will have to discriminate against Black people. Such a practice makes it near impossible for people to take Blacks seriously. Blacks are tired of being saddled with a negative identity. In developing their own identity, Blacks believe they will be able to choose their own way in the world.

It Starts With Change:
The Development Of
A New Identity

Developing a new identity starts with change. It can be as subtle as a name change. Names are, of course, culture-based. Names often reflect heritage. Many people inherent names from their biological parents. Even female children are often assigned full names from their biological mothers. There is nothing wrong with it. In fact, it is a part of many traditions. These names have significant meaning. Names individualize people, making them unique.

Names give out all sorts of information: your geographical location and point of origin, for example. Your history, heritage, and culture, region, language, and the dialect spoken, can be determined simply by stating your name. Unfortunately, it is our assigned names we more than often need to grown into. In essence, the purpose of assigning names to people is to let the world know who they are as an individual and as a whole.

Black people develop names to give their avowed identities significant meaning. Their names can consist of a word or words known or distinguished from other people or languages. English, European, Hispanic, Arabian, Native American, and African names can be used in combination to derive a new name. Jamal, Shaquan or Shaquana, and Laquisha and Donesha are prime examples of names that sound right and true for today's Blacks.

For the most part, Black Americans develop their own names to better describe the way they and their people are evolving in the world. The name Sharonda clearly shows evolutionary signs of progression. The name is a combination of two Eurocentric names. Sharon and Rhonda are combined to produce a name that sounds authentically Black. However, names can only be combined in so many ways before you stumble onto names from other cultures. So, Black names can be found abroad, especially when using a language-base predominant in the world. Meanwhile, names like Tyreke are of Jamaican origin and reflect the persistence and presence of African and Caribbean culture. Each has strong influence among Blacks in American society. By the way, the name Tyreke means "love."

Curiously, names like Terry, Christopher, and Brock are typically found in Western cultures. These names are Eurocentric and reflect Europe or its people, institutions, and cultures. When immigrants arrive in Western cultures, they often adopt Eurocentric names to show their willingness or eagerness to assimilate. Many want to be assimilated and quickly. This way, differences can be minimized or eliminated. Their goal is to be absorbed into the cultural mainstream. Then, they can contribute their knowledge to the scheme of Western production.

Name changes can have staggering effects on Western society. It's a direct measurement of how productive a society has become. When citizens, not just immigrants, are proud to be a part of a country, they will patronize it by adopting names that better characterize its legacies. They work in favor of preserving the status quo. They will also work to preserve traditional values and social customs. The practice helps to legitimize their intentions as US citizens.

When citizens take on new names and immigrants refuse to change their names, it's usually a sign that a country is unfair in its treatment of its citizens. In the 1950's and 1960's, for example, many Whites from the younger generation took on the names of Native Americans. Called Hippies, they refused to accept the social and political values of their elders. As a result of their country's bigoted policies, they proclaimed a belief in universal peace and love. Hippies often dressed unconventionally, lived communally, and used psychedelic drugs. These broad-minded individuals refused to accept conservatism and rebelled against the status quo.

As stated earlier, there is another movement underway, a conscious movement to reestablish a separate and distinct cultural system. The system will be reminiscent of a classic age or time when Blacks controlled their own economy, had political independence, and thriving communities. It will also have the orderliness of a complex social system. And with the younger generation vowing to develop a new identity, there will be substantial precedents for reestablishing a code of conduct.

As Black communities are reestablished, members will begin to form a code of conduct. This community code will consist of unwritten rules concerning acceptable standards of behavior. The idea is to maintain order in the community. I cannot stress the importance of community members developing their own fashion sense as part of acquiring an avowed identity. Changes in fashion are universal truths. But, it's more like developing an identity over time rather than making abrupt changes in your personal appearance. In essence, your style of dress becomes a part of who you've become as a person.

Once Blacks emerge into their new identity, there is often a fashion change. Conscious Blacks tend to wear items of cloths or an article of clothing that reflect part of their struggle or a positive affirmation, declaring something true or unique about themselves: their attitude, point of view, or lifestyle, for example. Dr. Cornel West modeled himself after the eminent Negro scholar W. E. B. Du Bois. Du Bois was best known for wearing black clothing, which he believed symbolized his commitment to Black suffrage and their struggles to move forward. Dr. West's attire reflected the same level of excellence and commitment found among the top 10 percent of Black public intellectuals living during the early 1900's. His attire reflects generations of people who paved the way for his success.

Someone from Baltimore asked Dr. West what was he doing still wearing clothing he wore during the last Civil Rights movement? His reply was, "these are my cemetery cloths… I'm coffin ready…" are you ready to die for your cause? Cornel's outward appearance, which was very impressive, truly reflected his morals and personal values. Conscious Blacks also have a conception of the world that broadens their understanding of humanity or life itself. In focusing on resolving problems that affect our most vulnerable, they bring legitimacy to the movement.

On the other hand, conscious Black people tend to suffer from discrimination because their names often sound authentically Black. Jaden and Jaquan, inherently Black names are, as many Whites feel, arrogantly dismissive of Western culture. Whites often ask why stay in the West when, clearly, they choose not to assimilate in this way? Incidentally, Black people's desire to integrate is often ignored and considered threatening to the cultural mainstream. In fact, Western cultures are so hostile toward Blacks, especially Black Americans, making a name change could further disadvantage them. So then, why resist the dominant power structure? Why not take on Western traits or subscribe to other characteristics of Western society?

Whenever I ask that question, the answer is most always the same. Blacks would like to learn how to function independent from the tyranny of Western imperialism. Many feel subjugated by Whites. They're hurt by the fact that Whites arrogantly dismiss their continued pain and suffering. So, Blacks do what they can to resist the powers that be. And for them, it starts with small, subtle symbolisms like name changes.

Today, there are two main reasons why Blacks develop their own names. Some would like their children to have unique names, names with special meaning. Then there are those who choose to not conform to cultural expectations. They assign their children names that fit the social roles they envision for them at birth. They feel it is their civic duty to contribute their efforts to improving Blacks in American society. For that very reason, Blacks are more often assigned to lower social status.

What are some of the consequences for showing nonconformity? Blacks with unconventional names receive fewer callbacks after job interviews. They're more often stereotyped as being nonconformists even though most are quite productive. In grade school, they're labeled troublesome, delinquent, or antisocial. And, depending on the lifestyle, they're targeted for discrimination by peers and neighbors.

It's a terrible consequence of reality whenever anyone suffers indignity at the hands of others. But, to be constantly discriminated against by an oppressor can have a profound impact on the human psyche. The upside is Blacks who choose to not conform tend to live a balanced lifestyle. The downside is those who fail to find their way in society end up tormented as social outcaste. So, I guess the next question would be why not simply conform to cultural expectations?

When people conform to cultural expectations, they betray their principles. In the Western world, that means to act in ways that are contrary to your standards of moral reasoning. For example, Blacks would have to adopt the mentality of their oppressors. And that's not a problem for some. Some people discriminate against their own people just to gain social acceptance. Their reasoning for doing so is to reduce further conflict in their lives.

In contrast, young Blacks believe it to be an act of insanity to betray your own principles or be disloyal to your people by helping those who oppressed you. Therefore, Blacks who resist the status quo by assigning their children nonconforming names are, in fact, instigating change. Many believe they are doing their part by staying true to the cause. However, there are more Black people willing to conform than not.

Let's consider Black women who dye their hair blonde. Their behavior constitutes the extreme end of social conformity. Remember the old adage, blondes have more fun? According to a Google search, its means "men are more attracted to women with blonde hair and give them more attention." But how does that translate when living in a multicultural environment? A closer inspection reveals a deeper meaning. Here's the answer: Dominant society feel Blacks need to conform if they are looking to find social acceptance among Whites. In fact, you can clearly see that Black women tend to appropriate their hairstyles the same as or very similar to their oppressors. Why? They're under constant pressure to conform.

Sadly, there is enormous pressure for people to conform in Western society. So Blacks who understand they can never be the same as or share in similarity to their oppressors, do what they can to fit in. They adopt methods to gain acceptance, especially on valued dimensions. This means adopting the speech patterns of their oppressors, taking on their gestures, mimicking their appearances, in a deliberate and exaggerated way to discourage their oppressors from taking predatory actions against them. Their hairstyles, fashions, and mannerisms are mimicked just to find peace of mind.

Most times, their expectations are haunted by their skin color. This problem has a direct connection to colorism, which started during the period of slavery. Some Blacks feel like they have skin color that is too dark. Some believe that regardless of how acculturated they become, they will never find acceptance in the cultural mainstream. Instead, many bleach their skin in an exaggerated way to achieve Whiteness. For example, more Black women are bleaching their skin today and at the risk of being rejected by members of their own race. Black celebrities like Lil Kim, Nicki Minaj, even Actress Tempestt Bledsoe, bleached their skin in what many Black people felt was the rejection of their racial identity. Their self-loathing causes complications for many Blacks who choose to maintain their identity.

Still, an increasing amount of Blacks continue to acculturate themselves and just to gain social acceptance. Sadly, more Blacks continue to breed out the melanin found in their skin. They're taking on White and light skin partners in order to give birth to lighter skin children. There is even a minority of Blacks who refuse to breed in fear of bearing dark-skinned children. They often fall prey to malicious stereotypes. The problem is they continue to define themselves in ways that hurt development toward more complete, modern social conditions.

They're also burden by their dark-skin. They believe that dark-skinned Blacks are intellectually inferior to light-skinned Blacks and White people in general. In fact, many would rather have a tubal ligation or vasectomy opposed to having dark-skinned children. Curiously, quite a few Blacks refer to skin bleaching and add-mixing as a lack of consciousness.

The Notion Of
Restoring Integrity

It became quite popular to develop names in the 1980's. It was especially true for the younger generation. The idea was to create names that restored integrity to a downtrodden people. Many Blacks were oppressed and losing confidence in their own humanity. The problem was Blacks felt like they were in an oppressive situation from which there was no escape.

They felt considerably disadvantaged under the government's control. The government was oppressive to

Blacks. Many were forced to endure chronic life conditions. Poverty imposed considerable stress on them. And, they were tired of being typecast as a result of the inappropriateness of their past situation in America. In this way, Blacks needed to have a new identity, not ascribed to them as had been the case in previous generations, but one they felt was right or true for them.

Many young Blacks refused to follow African tradition. They considered it to be backwards in terms of its customs and beliefs. They felt more likely to be typecast because of their Africanism as they once were during chattel slavery. Others wanted out of poverty. And Africa could not offer them a way out. More Blacks were disturbed over the notion of being socially rejected by Africans in the West. And, well, Blacks were never accepted by Westerners. Still, there were those who resisted the idea of finding social acceptance for the aforementioned reasons. For them, developing their own identity was the only way to resolve their situation.

But, in order to understand the importance of developing their own names, an awakening had to occur. You don't just wake up in the morning and say, "Hey, I'm going to make up a new name for myself." "It will make me feel better." There has to be certain events repeating in a person's life before anyone would assume a name change thus establishing a new identity. For example, it can be the integrity that comes with belonging to a conscious movement or the shame of bearing great guilt that gives rise to a complete awakening. Dr. John Henrik Clark watched a theatrical play called Pillar of Society written by Henrik Ibsen. It impacted his life so profoundly that Dr. Clark changed his middle name from Henry or Henrik. For Dr. Clark, the name change gave his identity significant meaning. It was that added influence in Dr. Clark's life that made his genius even better.

So what's the first step in developing an avowed identity? The first step is to become conscious. To achieve consciousness, you have to fully appreciate the importance of change. How do I stress the importance of appreciating change? Actually, it's the idea of change that needs to be considered. You have to first recognize and understand that the quality of life in your surroundings is not beneficial. And last, you must become well-informed on problems that affect not only you but your people's surroundings. That comes with fortifying your knowledge through education or information. Hopefully, you will then be able to take up activities with like-minded people and, together, work to instigate change in your environment. After all, achieving self-awareness is the first step to becoming conscious. If you fail to see the value, relevance, or do not take interest in your own situation, you will not be able to effect change in any situation.

Think about the current state of affairs in America. Blacks are the current victims of official murders, sanctioned by state government. If you have no idea why this is happening in America, it is because dominant society believes diversity will lead to the genetic annihilation of the White race. Imagine the predicament their psychopathology imposes on Black folk.

Blacks were unlawfully removed from their former nations. They were forced to live life as slaves in a hostile environment. They lost cultural and psychological contact with their traditional societies. Thus, they lost important cultural characteristics that, essentially, were not replaced by those in dominant society. As a result, everything Black people know about their history was ascribed to them by White people. I recently said, in my last book, The Color of Our Souls, that:

> The problem with being oppressed by America is you have to rely on White people to tell you who you are. Your story, history, and culture rest with a people completely without mercy. That means they can tell you whatever they want; and, you would have to accept it as the truth.

Now imagine the dilemma Blacks must confront today. Utterly frightful, don't you think? Black people's fate is uncertain, not just here in America, but throughout the world. In order for them to achieve change in Western thinking, they must control their own narrative. That means they must give their own account of history in the order in which they saw it happen. That process often begins by educating yourself on your history, culture, and heritage. It also tends to involve reconnecting to your former countries or its people, institutions, and culture. The idea is to raise your awareness about your own history or broaden your understanding of the world. Achieving awareness will help to reduce the chance of your government hiding the truth from you.

Reestablishing A
Sense of Pride

People often develop a great sense of pride from establishing their own identity. It's the universe's way of correcting cultural discrepancies between distinctly different cultural systems. When Black people develop names for their children, it removes the negativity ascribed to them by their oppressors. It's also their way of finding, taking back, and keeping their right and true identity. In fact, it forces White people to respect the importance and value of Black people or their lives, efforts, and achievements. In this way, Whites learn to refrain from violating their humanity. Thus for Black people, having their own identity will teach Whites how to behave, think, and feel toward them as a whole.

The civil rights movement taught Americans the importance of having their own identity. It was a time in which Blacks came into their own rights. Previously called Negros, the Black pride movement emphasized self-awareness for those who, in effect, achieved pride from developing a new racial identity. Black pride, as a movement, encouraged Negros to stay committed to the fight and embrace their African heritage. Today, Black people are reaffirming the importance of their position in society. Unfortunately, identity-pride has no bearing on whether Black people will achieve respect or acceptance in mainstream culture.

Although people might achieve a secure sense of self simply by establishing their own identity, they may experience hostility that exists outside their system of support. Conflicting values, morals, and behaviors can make it difficult to achieve core competence among the cultural mainstream. However, having pride in your own identity can help raise the level of awareness needed to achieve full consciousness. It can also diminish the burden of shame and doubt.

We are a half century past the Civil Rights era and people can see that Blacks have greater self-concepts than their White comparison counterparts. Such positivity comes from removing labels other people ascribed to them. Most people ascribe cultural characteristics to Blacks based on generalizations they've made about them, their people, or culture. The idea of dispelling cultural stereotypes is what gave rise to the notion of choosing to assign their children names they feel are right or true for them. And, I must say, they're arousing strong emotional reactions in people for doing so.

What We Can Do To Resolve It

What we can do to help Black people resolve the problem of choosing an identity is raise self-awareness. It's a long, arduous process. But, it leads to the development of racial consciousness.

First, you should understand that searching for an avowed identity means Black people are tired of having their freedoms and responsibilities restricted by the dominant power structure. In fact, people consider it to be a way of protesting the act of paternalism. How so? The act of having your identity avowed is a practice on the part of a people who are pressuring the dominant power structure to change its position on people they oppress for their supposed best interest. The practice encourages Western governments to give Black people more freedom and responsibility. It reinforces the notion that they have, in some way, been oppressed by their government; and, the terms of their condition are no longer acceptable. Thus, it tells other nations that Black people continue to endure oppression.

Second, the search for an avowed identity also means that Black people are willing to break from cultural expectations. They are willing to uphold a higher level of moral commitment, living by a moral code that will set them apart from Western culture, especially on valued dimensions. They believe that their new identity will help them adapt to live under the overwhelming stress of oppression. That having a new identity will help them to dispel some of the negative stereotypes that characterize Black people as inferior.

And third, the establishment of an avowed identity shows the sacrifice and commitment Black people are willing to make to achieve racial consciousness. Their level of consciousness also shows that Blacks are a remarkable people. Over the centuries, they've shown their ability to adapt, owing principally to their resilience in their quest for equality. Oddly enough, having an avowed identity puts people under the false impression that Black people are looking to achieve sovereignty as an independent nation. That idea is far from the truth for most Black people. They're simply requesting the right to have a politically independent state.

An *avowed identity* affirms that the set of characteristics we recognize as belonging uniquely to a person is right or true for them, making up his or her demeanor for life. It's different from *ascribed identity*, which is based on cultural stereotypes Western society imposes on people they oppress. People usually develop an interest in establishing an avowed identity after learning about cultural problems that affect their circumstances.

Avowed identities are essential features in instigating change in the cultural attitude. It forces the public to recognize or acknowledge their prejudice toward a particular person or people. It can also bring about improvement to one's self-concept. It makes it easier or possible for a person to accept who they are as a whole. Avowing one's identity is not necessarily an act of protest, either. It works to show that a person is no longer a victim of their circumstances. In this case, the person raises his or her self-awareness to the point of consciousness.

It's the conscious-minded folk who will raise the awareness of others. The conscious will continue to do what they've been doing and that is to protest, inspire, and lead in the fight for justice. The time for change is now, yesterday, and always when we're ready to create and establish equality and justice for everyone. It starts at home, with you. Why? You have the responsibility to take action for your wellness and not try to pass emotional instability on to someone else. It may not seem true. But, you are ultimately responsible for every aspect of your life.

How do you achieve self-awareness? You must first be the willing receipt of acceptance without protest. Acceptance is an indication that you agree change is needed. That is to say, you have to agree that there is a problem that affects not only your circumstances but our most vulnerable. Then you must be willing to treat acceptance (i.e., the education or information given) as the realization of that fact or truth.

The last step in this process is, you must take action. The first step is to fortify your understanding of your situation. It is done through the use of education or information. You will also need to seek out like-minded people. Being surrounded by people who share the same or similar views and opinions as you is critical to your intellectual development. It will give you the mental and moral courage to commit to whatever it takes to instigate change.

In the next chapter, we will discuss whether young Blacks who refuse to learn are having an identity crisis or taking a political stance. By examining such fascinating questions, you will learn more about the struggles they endure at the hands of their oppressors.

Chapter 5
An Identity Crisis Or A Political Stance

Refusing to Learn

Once you know who you are, you don't have to worry anymore.

Nikki Giovanni (1943 - Present)

It's been said that Black Americans are undergoing an identity crisis. Blacks have struggled for centuries in search of their own identity. For the most part, Black people would like to know who they are, where they come from, and what contributions their ancestors made to the world. Unfortunately, many may never learn.

Over the centuries, Blacks have undergone a few identity changes. Perhaps, the largest identity change occurred during the period of chattel slavery when Black people completely lost their identity. It would take them more than 349 years to evoke memories of their lost identity.

Most of us understand that people will undergo an identity crisis whenever there is a cultural and psychological disconnection between their former nations; and, that contact has not been replaced by those of the larger society. In this way, the essential features that make Black Americans inherently African were removed from them and not replaced by those of the larger, more dominant society. In practice, when the larger, more dominant society forces the smaller, less dominant culture into a marginal standard of living, it puts greater pressure on the marginal group to change. And that's just what happened; the lack of contact between Whites and Blacks placed considerably more stress on Blacks to change. So Blacks did just that; they changed!

Blacks changed their way of life. In fact, they adapted to a new way of living. Many made due under the system of segregation, during which time the US Government segregated all public venues to include schools, residential areas, public parks, theaters, pools, cemeteries, asylums, jails, and residential homes. Historically Black colleges and universities (HBCU's) like Howard University in Washington, D.C. and Fisk University in Nashville, Tennessee were created by Blacks to compensate them for the lack of available resources. From about 1890 to the 1920's, and as a result of education, Black communities flourished all over America.

The end of the Victorian Era (1890 - 1901) marked a new period of time for Black Americans. During this time, the second largest identity change occurred for Black people. Blacks came into their own right, recognized as one of the most successful racial groups in America. Black Americans began to experience changes in personal appearance and mannerisms. Called the Gay Nineties, it gave rise to the happy-go-lucky Negro, the Black business professional, the beginning of the suffragette movement, and the birth of ragtime music (1895). An African-American composer and pianist, Scott Joplin, became renowned for his ragtime compositions and was crowned the King of Ragtime.

Black communities developed and prospered all across America. Black people would come to build their own business industries, public facilities, transportation resources, community centers, grocery stores, et cetera. Many would thrive and flourished for years under the system of segregation. Unfortunately, the US Government sought to remove all aspects of the Black community in a way Blacks would suffer for generations.

Tensions built up as Blacks became more prosperous in the United States. Whites continued to exercise their power to completely segregate Blacks from dominant society. Only now, Whites were angry. Race riots and massacres ensued across America. One of the most disturbing cases in United States history, one of significant importance, took place on May 31 to June 1 of 1921, at the Greenwood District in Tulsa, Oklahoma. This attack was carried out on the ground and from the air, destroyed more than 35 square blocks of residential and business developments at a time when it was the wealthiest Black community in America, known as Black Wall Street. The government continued to maldistribute its resources. The entire process left Black Americans marginal.

Today, Whites ignore every aspect of Black people to include their marginality. And, many people believe Blacks are disorganized and would like to destroy the unity White people created for themselves. Oddly, it's not that Black people are against White unity. In fact, many Blacks are upset over the maldistribution of resources that continue to prevent them from reaching full equality in America. They are also visibly upset over acculturating people who ignore their personal obligations to uplift their own race, especially those who are willing to relinquish their racial identity to move into dominant White society.

Marginalization is what caused Blacks to endure feelings of alienation and identity loss. This period in time is what made Blacks undergo several important name changes. Names like boy, Nigger, Negro, Colored or Colored Person, Black American, Person of Color, Afro-American, and African American (with and without the hyphen), can be said to show cultural progress or, quite the opposite, a considerable amount of confusion and anxiety for a people.

Out of the confusion were born various ages. These ages gave way to events that would bring about hope and inspiration to Black people. For example, the age of slavery gave rise to church hymns. Called Negro spirituals, these inspirational religious songs originated from oral tradition, especially traditions arising from the Black American slave experience. Slaves used these songs to communicate information secretly and briefly to one another. Many of these spirituals were codified to help fleeing slaves escape from slavery to freedom. For most Black Americans, the constant struggle for freedom became quite unsettling, thus weighing heavily on their minds.

Do you remember names like Negro and Colored, leading up to African American? These names were attempts at developing and establishing their own identity. Well, the result is there's a generational split between younger and older Black Americans. For example, some members of the older generation are comfortable being called Negro. They were born under the assertion that Black people were Negros, many, free Negros. It was written on their birth certificates, accepted as formal English in America, and was spoken as the gospel in church. In fact, it was viewed by people around the world as politically correct (PC) language. The problem with using the term Negro to identify Blacks is it's too easily mocked.

Variations of the name Negro began to appear in the early beginnings of American history. Nigger was a variant used to intimidate Blacks in a way intended to make them feel ashamed, embarrassed, or regretful. Other, more colorful names that were given by Whites appeared to trivialize or shame them as well. Many of these names were so trivializing, they often created racial tensions and hostility. All the conflict eventually led to a period of identity confusion whereby Black people became uncertain about who they were, what they were all about, and where they were headed in life. In fact, some Blacks continue to lack in self-assurance or confidence as a result.

Continuous conflict and tension led to a highly stressful crisis for Black people. Homicide, suicide, family abuse, and substance abuse quickly became a normative influence of acculturating Blacks. Basically, any Blacks who tried to succeed in life were greatly affected by Whites and their impetus toward contact or social interaction. And with racial tensions high, there appeared to be no plans in place to create a resolution for Black people, at least not one foreseeable in the near future.

It wasn't until 1952, when Malcolm X entered the fight for social justice that then-Negros would begin to embrace the term Black as a racial identity. It was Brother Malcolm who pushed the Black identity as a political agenda during the Civil Rights movement. Other than Malcolm and the Nation of Islam, it was unpopular to identify as Black. The term Black was not consecrated by the church thus was considered to be an extremely bad or offensive label. In fact, it was viewed as deliberately defiant of specific religious precepts.

Later, the late great Pan-African Kwame Ture (Stokely Carmichael) empowered audiences by giving his Black Power speech (1966), a speech that he delivered during the Civil Rights movement in the United States. But, it wouldn't be until music recording legend James Brown released his hit song, "Say It Loud, I'm Black and I'm Proud," that Black people would truly embrace their identity.

That's right, James Brown's song, Say It Loud, I'm Black and I'm Proud, was awe-inspiring. Perhaps heavily influenced by Malcolm X and, later, by Kwame Ture, the song was so awe-inspiring, it made Whites humble and slightly afraid. In the same sense, it gave Black people the courage to think of themselves in broader cultural dimensions. They would also begin to reject the customary way in which dominant society considered them.

Young Blacks began to take pride in their identity. They refused to learn or be influenced by Whites. They rejected the use of terms like Colored and Negro and embraced their new found identity, identifying as Black American. Other movements appeared during the Civil Right Era, political movements like Black power, Black Nationalism, and the Black Panther Party, were formed to ensure that Black people would receive equal protection under the law.

These activist groups took vigorous and sometimes aggressive action in pursuing political means or social ends. These groups also worked together with other activist groups to bring about specific, often radical change in social, economical, and political policies and practices. As part of their agenda, and in their spare time, the Black Panther Party created early morning breakfast and community-based after school programs. They also created recreational programs to encourage and enhance the health and wellness of young Blacks residing in urban areas of American society. And for the first time since the Roaring Twenties, Blacks began to take pride in their racial identity.

In the United States, the Black Pride Movement was created in direct response to White supremacy, especially in terms of correcting the cultural legacies and burdens of slavery. In fact, during the early days of the Civil Rights movement, the agenda was not about racial integration but bringing about equality to segregation. The initial problem was that the government maldistrubuted most of the major resources in the country so that Blacks could not reach full equality or would be reduced to a permanent underclass. Resources like mineral, wealth, labor, capital, and material assets have always been withheld from Blacks to ensure their servility.

The Black pride movement encouraged Black people to celebrate their cultural achievements and embrace their African heritage. Many behaviors had to be unlearned in order for them to accept their Africanism. Blacks had to unlearn Western instruction. Specifically, they had to rid their minds of the knowledge or memory that Western civilization was taught as truthful or correct.

Many Blacks relied heavily on Western history as a matter of principle. However, they had to unlearn it in a way that taught them much of their history was Whitewashed to hide the truth, especially the truth about their African heritage. Blacks also had to learn or accept education on a global level, coming from a critical perspective of Black historians who challenged basic assumptions about Whites and their racial policies.

W. E. B. Du Bois, Carter G. Woodson, and James Turner are accredited with founding the first school of Africana studies to describe a global approach to Black studies. They were the first scholars to go into a previously uncharted or unclaimed territory with the purpose of exploring it and settling it. James Turner received credit for naming Black studies the Africana Studies and Research Center at Cornell. Afterwards, he took his place as the founding director.

The problem with the Africana Studies and Research Center at Cornell was the lack of support it received from the academy of academics. Then in the 1960's, and born out of the Civil Rights and Black Power Movements, students from various collegiate institutions protested against and demanded that administrators create programs so students could earn degrees in Black Studies. Courses in African and African American Studies were among the first to be taught in colleges and universities across America.

The three wise-men, Drs. John Henrik Clark, Ivan Gladstone Van Sertima, and Yosef Alfredo Antonio Ben-Jochannan, were the foremost authorities in the field of African studies. These educators were responsible for helping Black people attain a higher intellectual, moral, or spiritual development by improving the quality of information given to Blacks about Blacks. Chancellor J. Williams (1898 - 1992), an African-American sociologist as well as an historian and writer, was noted for his work on African civilizations prior to encounters with Europeans. His major work includes The Destruction of Black Civilization. Even after his death, Chancellor Williams continues to remain a key figure on the topic of Afrocentrism.

Uncovering The Unspoken Truth

Uncovering the unspoken truth to which I mean pointing out whitewashing in American history can be daunting. But for whom? Today in lecture halls on college and university campuses across America, much of the Black student discourse centers on speaking or uncovering the unspoken truth. Black students uncover many aspects of history not readily talked about in college lectures. For the Black student, what was once thought to be creditable lectures given by notable scholars and professors is nothing more than racism left unexamined in past textbooks.

Many of these college professors are not attuned to the nuances of racism put forth in student textbooks. Hence, many of their lectures are racist unbeknown to them as offensive phrases are often cloaked in the tradition of excellence and under the authority of language. Professors, many bothered by utterance of student responses, are forced to unlearn insensitivity to Black people and stop their traditional way of speaking and writing.

Even I have a story I consider to be an important influence of not only this chapter but the book in its entirety. Toward the end of my sophomore year, I repeated a course on African American history. Only this time, the course was taught by a White (that's right, a White) history professor. We suffered the loss of our Black history professor, Mrs. Faulkner. So, he served as her temporary replacement.

Mrs. Faulkner was special. She was the first professor who gave me a grade of "F." It wasn't the F-grade that made her special but the lecture that came with it. In one lesson, Mrs. Faulkner taught me how to become a successful student; and, I mean a genuine college student! From that point onward, it was nothing for me to take a course in African studies, at least one course a semester. The goal was to take any course that had a writing track. In this way, I could better myself.

So this time, I'm sitting in class, and thinking to myself, "I am not going to learn anything from this White history professor." Other students refused to quiet down as the entire class was visually disturbed by his mere presence. He sat calmly and tried to chime in on a discussion the class was having about him. In order to quiet down the class, I turned the discussion into a philosophical debate. I raised the argument of whether a White man should teach an African studies course at the freshman level. We debated the proposition or suggestion, argued the affirmative and the negative. Boy, day one was interesting to say the least.

Two students left the course right away. Perhaps, they had more sense than anyone else. I considered the course to be an opened opportunity for any intellectuals willing to accept the challenge. The next 15 semester hours would prove to be challenging.

I tried to be optimistic about him. That's why I initiated the debate. But in day two of the course, it became apparent that this professor was going to be a challenge. He did not take kindly to my considerations nor did he have a desire to teach African American history. Himself, a historian, it was a course he was qualified to teach. A job was available, a course was open, so he taught it; or, dare I say, he took it.

He proceeded to teach us about the cultural legacies and burdens of American slavery, which included involunt-ary servitude, the colonization of Africans in the Americas, and how Abraham Lincoln freed the slaves. The class was intelligent enough to ask him questions he didn't know. A few of us held the class together by filling in the blanks for students. Collectively, we could proctor the course from where we sat. We all agreed that we would not learn from him as his continuance with whitewashing history wore sorely on us.

We, as a class, challenged the professor throughout the entire semester. If we were pigeonholed into completing the course, then he was going to learn a thing or two about African American history or Black Americans to say the least. Our goal was to help him unlearn habits that would allow racism to exist in books unexamined. He did not understand the implications of racism in textbooks since he, himself, was a racist. He did not have a problem with statements made in the book that were whitewashed or had racist overtones.

He use derogatory terms like "Negro," which in today's society is dated and offensive. Other terms and phrases like "you people," "culturally dependent," "subordinate groups," and "inferior or inferiority" had overtones of malice in its meaning. In fact, the professor viewed life through the aesthetic lens of White male supremacy. So, we made him choose his own language and avoid racist content as a matter of practice. We made him suffer through every offensive phrase we encountered during class discussion. And we criticized him whenever he hesitated to give credit to Black people when appropriate.

Our refusing to learn racist material from a professor who learned to present racist speeches before a predominantly Black student-audience as a traditional way of thinking influenced who we were, what we were all about, and where we were heading as scholars. The problem is society expects Black people to conform to cultural expectations. But that semester, we turned a potentially racist experience into an intellectual exercise. What a healthy response to a biased yet traditional way of thinking.

In past years, and as part of his superiority complex, the professor learned to be insensitive, not only to Blacks but Hispanics as well. He had a biased and traditional way of thinking and writing. It was his lack of sensitivity in our presence that bothered me. I learned to pick and choose my battles with him. He, on the other hand, had to learn how to be selective of the problems, arguments, and debates that he became accustomed to as a matter of habit, practice, and tradition.

Three semesters later, I continued working at the community college after transferring to a four-year liberal arts college. I continued to maintain rapport with this history professor only to be discouraged about letting any White person teach a course in African studies, at any academic level, whether or not he or she was qualified. Why? At a time when Black people are searching for their rightful or true identity, the image projected or the type of energy given could very well lower their self-concept and esteem.

History has shown us that White people, especially conservative Republicans, will make coordinated attempts to hide unpleasant truths about African American history. They warn Black people that White people are not con-cerned with nor do they choose to help Blacks, especially in a social, economical, or political context.

A Political Stance Taken

There's no denying. Young Blacks are making a political stance. They are refusing to learn from their oppressors. They are firm and unwavering in the search for their own identity. They are committed to establishing the balance of power between cultural systems. And their eagerness to tell their story strengthens their resolve.

Certainly, it is true that Black people are slightly disturbed or emotionally affected by racism and White supremacy. With the amount of racial tension and hostility occurring over the centuries, it's no wonder why Black people exist in a state of confusion. They suffered identity loss, mental, physical, and sexual trauma, multigenerational trauma, and a continuance of neglect. But they have not been disturbed deeply enough to change their behavior or way of thinking. In this way, they have been resilient in their efforts to hold on to what's left of their identity. And, that's the problem. "We may bend a little; but, we don't break!"

What should be left over are a broken people. Blacks are badly hurt by grief or misfortune. Yet, they remain steadfast in their decision to end the suffering that governs their lives. They continue to engage in social and political activism, sometimes taking on vigorous and aggressive actions in pursuing both ends of the political spectrum. And with the hopes of bringing their suffering to an abrupt end, they remain firmly fixed on human rights violations that affect the body of politics and the partisan aspects of political government. Any hint of political activism, especially insofar as removing power relationships from the right-of-center, occurs for purely political ends.

The purpose of political activism is not to gain some calculated advancement. The only reason Blacks develop tactics and strategies to gain political power in government is for the purpose of ending their oppression. Black people made considerable progress in recently years.

Blacks have made small but notable progress in the fight for equal rights. There have been other advancements in American society as well. These advancements include the rights to freedom, justice, and equality, freedom of opinion and expression, the right to work, to achieve a quality education, and many more human rights achievements that are considered by most societies to automatically belong to everyone thus should be upheld without prejudice or discrimination.

One of the great progressions or advancements of Black people was the understanding that not only their basic (civil) rights were being violated but their human rights were being directly violated. These violations are what sparked the push to not learn from the very people who oppressed them. Dominant society disturbed or interrupted Black lives in a way that subjugated them to a harsh or cruel form of domination. Blacks who have yet to take up political activism show their support for Black lives by refusing to learn from their oppressors. Yet, they continue to educate themselves in a way that renews hope and inspires a Black awareness movement.

This Black awareness movement is not new by any sense of the imagination. It is a grassroots anti-oppression movement that seeks awareness of Black people and their true identity. And much like what happened in South Africa during the mid-1960's, it was a way for conscious-minded Black folk to put their arm on those who were unaware.

Conscious Blacks forced awareness on Black people who refused to consider the truth about their own quality of living in American society. Many, themselves victims, are the survivors of systemic oppression that result from a political vacuum created by jailing and murdering Black Americans, Black Nationalists, and Pan-African leadership during and after the Civil Rights movement (1960's). This conscious Black movement will help bring awareness to more Black people and the world around them.

It's not enough to be well-informed about what is going on in the world or about the latest developments in a sphere of activity. More conscious-mined Black people are starting to commit their efforts to helping Blacks learn their true identity. It's nothing personal. Each and every human should know who they are, where they come from, and what important contributions their ancestors made in this world. Why? It's a natural progression of human evolution. It is also a quality of humans, that is to say, the qualities considered as a whole to be characteristic of humans.

What We Can Do To Resolve It

What we can do to resolve society's problem with its confusion about Blacks and their position in life is to continue doing what we've been doing. Why? There is hope even in our fragile White supremacist society that life will improve for Blacks. Unfortunately, like any mental health disorder, there is currently no cure for White supremacy. In this way, White supremacy is an incurable disease, one of the mind, body, and soul. However, and given more time, we may see a cure. But for now, like any good psychiatrist knows, mediation, much like talking therapy, only helps people cope with the disease.

However, there are political movements underway as we speak and radical change taking place. As young Black males refuse to learn, we're beginning to understand that they are making a political stance against oppression, further deepening the movement. The need to search for a new identity is a testament of their political views or beliefs.

Blacks endured quite a few problems with society, involving the loss of their identity. Hence, they've undergone quite a few identity changes. Name changes like boy, nigger, Negro, Colored Person, Afro-American, Person of Color, African American (with and without the hyphen) and more commonly, Black American summarizes the amount of changes Blacks endured just to establish their presence in American society. Yet, they continue to search for an identity that's right or true for them, putting Whites under the assertion that Blacks suffer from identity-confusion.

Thanks to music recording legend James Brown, Black American just might be their final stance. His famous recording song, Say it Loud, I'm Black and I'm Proud, reinvigorated an entire movement, taking it to a whole new level. But like any movement in a society governed by White supremacy, Blacks will never be satisfied with their identity without knowing their true history, and I mean all of it!

The problem is, and has always been, the concept of refusing to learn is considered a sign of marginality. Young Blacks refusing to learn in American society created a political vacuum. The results were many Blacks were jailed and murdered for no apparent reason than being young, Black and, in many cases, gifted. From that point onward, political discussions between Whites and Blacks would be completely lacking. In this way, White supremacy proves to be a disease of the soul, a problem so deep that its extent is not visible. In fact, White supremacy is so deeply rooted in evil, many people, and not just Black people, believe we are now in a situation of apparently unending awfulness. What we need to do about it is continue on with what we've been doing. And that is to encourage greater effort, enthusiasm, or optimism in order to stimulate the nation into political action, especially in creating a balance of power between cultural systems.

In this chapter, we have seen how refusing to learn can be mistaken for identity confusion. What many people consider to be an identity crisis, at closer inspection, turns out to be a political stance taken by a people who, for the most part, are tired of being oppressed. In the next chapter, we will take a look at what happens in the age of consciousness. It is a necessary discovery we must understand in order to balance out our discussion on refusing to learn. Afterward, we will have a meaningful discussion on arriving at your true identity.

Chapter 6
In The Age Of Consciousness

Never forget that intelligence rules the world and ignorance carries the burden. Therefore, remove yourself as far as possible from ignorance and seek as far as possible to be intelligent.

Marcus Mosiah Garvey (1887 – 1940)

Which era ushered in the age of consciousness? I'm not referring to that period in time when consciousness developed out of necessity. Although, it seems that the need to be conscious is ever present. I'm talking about when consciousness became fashionable, a style of intelligence popular with the people. Perhaps, it began with Former President Barack Obama, who renewed the hope and aspirations of countless Americans. The most educated President to be seated in the Oval Office since Abraham Lincoln, President Obama inspired Americans to think of life in broader cultural dimensions.

There were also intellectual greats like Dr John Henrik Clark, Dr. Ivan Gladstone Van Sertima, and Dr. Yosef Ben-Jochannan, who I call the three wise-men. They were the foremost authority on African history. They inspired entire movements. There were also public intellectuals Dr. Cornel West and Dr. Henry Louis Gates, Jr. who were so brilliant and gifted in their speech, they were the living embodiment of intelligence.

Certainly, there were other intellectuals like Michael Eric Dyson and newcomer Dr. Joy DeGruy whose public lectures were so charismatic, they possessed great powers of charm and influence. And who can forget comedian

Bill Cosby with his hit television series The Cosby Show and A Different World. Both shows had Black Americans aspire to greatness. These legends instilled a new found sense of consciousness in not only Black people but people from various walks of life. They displayed such exuberance over education that people understood their boundaries were endless so long as they strived to achieve.

But somewhere in the dark, unsuspecting gloom of the new millennium, dawn a new motivation. It appeared to function independent of academics and was invested in deep compassion for others. This awakening was characterized by a quest for truth and justice for every American, especially our most vulnerable. It awakened Americans suddenly and after first term President Donald Trump wreaked havoc in his wake. These people refer to themselves not as conscious-minded Black people but *woke* and informed citizens.

The rest of this chapter discusses the duality that exists between two mental states. Unconsciousness and consciousness are states of mental awareness that function at various levels of society.

What Is Consciousness?

Consciousness is awareness of one's surroundings. It occurs when a person becomes attuned to their environment. It is a long, arduous process. But, it can lead to greater self-awareness. For example, in this book, we're more concerned about why Black people are refusing to learn. People who share in this interest care about the wellness of our most vulnerable. But the decision to act on the resolutions found in this book is what we refer to as greater self-awareness or racial consciousness.

Racial consciousness is a complex undertaking. It is multiply determined not simply by several cultural factors. There are several cultural factors that operate simultaneously and interchangeably, setting it apart from other states of awareness. It occurs in that critical moment in time when a person self-actualizes. In that moment, he or she is driven to use his or her talents and potentials to better a situation not only for themselves but others. Many people are well-informed. But, when they take interest in critical issues that instigate change, they show their unselfish commitment to others. And, that selfless commitment is what we, in this book, call racial consciousness.

Racial consciousness varies in two fundamental ways: 1) being *woke* and informed on situations or the current state of affairs and 2), being well-informed on critical issues relating specifically to race, culture, and the politics of gender. After ascertaining some understanding of what is meant by racial consciousness, we will turn to its main states, paying special attention to how education or information can be achieved even in an altered state of awareness. Then we will end this chapter with a resolution section of which there will be a discussion resolving cultural problems surrounding the critical issue of race.

States of Mental Awareness:
Unconsciousness *vs.* Consciousness

Most people are cognizant of their situation and have a general awareness of what is happening to others in the world. Not many have the ability to act on the behalf of others. Some are preoccupied with their own problems. Others fail to care. Still, a few have the ability and will act on it. These states of awareness act in two fundamentally different ways: unconsciousness and consciousness. The mental states of unconsciousness can happen intentionally or unintentionally. But what connects these dimensions to a particular state of awareness is that both manifest in dissociated acts.

Unconsciousness, in the context of this book, is about being unaware of cultural problems surrounding the critical issue of race. It can be as simple as not acknowledging or failing to recognize a problem that can critically impact one's life. These problems have an immediate and strong effect on people, often Whites, but also Blacks, the poor, and our most vulnerable, in ways that cause anxiety or apprehension. The problem that causes this lack of consciousness produces apathy in the presence or anticipation of danger, harm, or failure. In essence, it is an emotional emptiness.

While some people are concerned with community building, others are more interested in exploiting its members and resources. Millions of people choose to be unconscious. It literately appears that they have an inability to feel normal, passionate human emotions. Not every person thinks in this way, but a lot of them do. In general, more people choose to remain unconscious than conscious. More of the unconscious are aware of critical problems that affect them but have become preoccupied with their own self-interests. Others, dare I say most, are struggling to exist in a hostile environment. They are preoccupied with their own struggles. The fact that it appears they are unable to respond emotionally to matters that concern their own wellness is an unconscious irony.

Though it is hard for people to consider that so many others are unconscious, several incidents throughout history prove that lack of awareness does exist. Let's consider voting priorities of the past. First, I understand why, at one point in time, Black people voted for the Republican Party. There is the misconception that the Civil War was waged to emancipate Blacks from chattel slavery. Then there is the false belief that Republicans actually care about people who fell under the tyranny of oppression.

Let's not forget the concept of capitalism, which Black Republicans subscribed to under the illusion of inclusion. American capitalism was the goal of Abraham Lincoln. Ending slavery simply gave him the means to get it done. Finally, let's not forget the Eugenics movement, which was a sterilization process that gave rise to segregation as an institution. Today, we have Black Republicans who voted for Donald Trump. Many of them followed Trump's policies in which he wanted to tease Black people apart from mainstream culture in the hopes of making them a permanent underclass.

Last, there are unique differences that exist between the conscious and unconscious. Mannerisms and often their style of dress are quite notable distinctions. Conscious Blacks tend to be stylishly graceful, show sophistication, and often have good taste in appearance and behavior. When this is true, it's more likely due to invested years in formal education.

For people who are intentionally unconscious, they have a different mindset. They have a combination of worldly wisdom, self-confidence and, on occasion, refinement. However, their main concern is self-preservation. They have a near instinctive need to do what is necessary to survive life in a hostile environment. But what's noticeable about them, and I mean the reason why we consider them to be unconscious, is their willingness to ignore the needs and wishes of others to succeed. That, and regardless of your efforts to familiarize them on topics of significant importance, they continue to show that their personal needs and wishes are more important than those of others.

Every scenario just given is a deliberate act of unconsciousness. In hindsight, you can imagine why Black people consider Black Republicans problematic. Do you now understand how they appear to show no due regard for the situation at-hand? The difference between someone who is intentionally unconscious and unintentionally unconscious is having the ability to learn from experience.

There is an unconscious irony for people who fail to realize or recognize cultural problems that affect who they are as a whole. These people are not generally aware that they lack consciousness. They often manifest their thoughts, feelings, and behaviors through dissociated acts. You cannot readily identify them by looking at their appearance, either. You usually have to engage in conversation in order to ascertain some understanding of who they are and how they think in terms of their outlook on life. After engaging in productive conversations, it becomes easier to determine the set of beliefs that affect their mindset. With limited exposure, it is unlikely you'd be accurate.

With keen insight, you can readily identify who is unconscious. Most unconscious people belong to a culture of consumption. They're often preoccupied with expending personal revenue in competition to show off, boast, or gloat about self-satisfactory achievements or someone else's misfortunes. Even if the above mentioned is untrue, and it's not, they tend not to care whether or not their position in society hurts another or others. Thus, they tend to be indifferent to others.

One hypothesis used to explain their indifference to others is that they believe society exists for the benefit of individual people who must not be constrained by government interventions or made subordinate to collective goals or interests. Thus, unconscious people are in pursuit of personal happiness and independence. What often stands out about them is their willful desires to socially exclude and persecute members of their own race.

Two States Of Consciousness

There are actually two states of consciousness we're concerned with in this chapter and throughout this book. Conscious and *woke* are both states of mental awareness. *Woke* is to become aware of an event or situation or make someone alert and active after being inactive and uninformed on important matters surrounding the issue of race. For example, the protester's pleas *woke* us to the situation. The person who is *woke* is more often your run of the mill, everyday, ordinary person both in behavior and appearance. Compared to consciousness, *woke* is more limited in awareness and its associative struggles harder to endure.

Reverend Martin Luther King, Jr. brought the word *woke* into the cultural mainstream on March 31, 1968. Dr. King gave a commencement address at the National Cathedral in Washington, DC where he challenged White Americans to live life in harmony or perish as fools. King gave Biblical accounts of vast empires that fell under the wrath of God. He pointed out that on many occasions Black people continued to be viewed as the White man's burden. That after slavery, Whites refused to situate Blacks so they could achieve an advantage. He felt that Whites benefited all others at the expense or consideration of Black people. His concerns would become apparent as he promised to bring the poor man's campaign to the doorsteps of the United States government. Dr. King utilized the word *woke* to alert White America to the fact that Black people would not rest until justice was achieved.

Today, the word *woke* resurfaced. This time, it was used by a younger crowd of Black protesters as a rational alternative to the word conscious. Apparently, the word conscious is dated and offensive to the younger generation. It has connotations that suggest education is a large part of becoming conscious. Many Blacks from the younger generation are refusing to learn. However, they also refuse to be the victims of police abuse and official murders sanctioned by state government.

They feel that education will lead them to greater hardship under the illusion of inclusion. They do not feel you need an education in order to reach full equality in American society. They believe that all people should receive equal treatment under the law regardless of race, color, or creed. Their generation, Generation Y, is unwilling to let the US Government continue its reign over Black people. Many are well aware of the crisis that exists in America. They understand that antiblack racism has taken a large toll on the Black population. And that Black Americans are challenged with fighting a nation that refuses to take accountability or assume responsibility for committing crimes against humanity.

I fear that what Generation Y failed to take into account is the amount of time it takes to fight inequality. The lack of education or information on the topic also caused their campaign to stagger during the first few years of protesting. Many protest groups continue to struggle today largely due to a lack of education or information. Members of these groups are eager to continue their campaign but often find themselves asking what's the next step in the political process of protesting? In this way, use of the word *woke* may very well be a sign that Black America has experienced a loss of awareness or, perhaps, preparedness.

A few protest groups found solace in larger, more stable protest groups. Others have simply taken their protest to the next level. These groups are led by experienced professionals who are well-equipped to take their supporters to the next level and beyond. In many cases, the awakened are becoming conscious-minded regardless of their will to resist education. They're finding themselves in positions where situation dictates and the cultural demands to save Black lives actually matter. Although use of the word *woke* has a few benefits, consciousness allows you to fully appreciate the importance of having keen awareness for what really matters.

Curiously, both states of awareness have unique qualities that make them special and worthy of note. Clearly, they operate differently. Since they do, yet often share goals, the two can learn to work cohesively as a united whole. Beyond excellence, to be *woke* or conscious in today's society means you are committed to Black suffering, or their pain and distress.

Staying Woke In The
Age Of Consciousness

Staying *woke* or aware of important issues after being politically unaware, asleep, or afraid to commit, or to inspire people to pledge their commitment in this way is commendable. Young Black males are making a conscientious decision to dedicate themselves to Black-themed issues. This near remarkable act of courage, commitment, and skill tends to happen while living in a hostile environment.

It's not easy for them to stay committed as they are fraught with substandard living conditions and the overwhelming stress of oppression. Many struggle to maintain their sense of right and wrong. They search for ways to maintain their awareness of important issues and focus on not falling into deviant behavior. Many endure trial-and-error methods of learning as they search for satisfactory solutions, usually by experimenting with alternatives and eliminating failures. For them, resisting formal education is, perhaps, the reason why they struggle. It's also likely the reason why they prefer to use the term *stay woke* instead of "stay conscious."

Young Blacks do not consider themselves to be conscious. *Stay woke* is the new catchphrase. It is a political term that resurfaced amid the official murders of young Blacks in America. It was the need to stay committed to the fight for justice that gave rise to this terminology. However, *stay woke* is not by any means formal English. It is a part of Black vernacular dialect. Its everyday usage means to maintain an awareness of race-related problems concerning social injustice.

Indeed *staying woke* is a state of awareness. It's a way of staying alert and active but not fully engaged in any one cause or movement. Racial consciousness involves another degree of commitment.

Conscious Blacks are backed by a rich tradition viewed as a set of precedents. Their devotion or dedication shows a stronger sense of awareness or sensitivity to race matters. You're talking about someone who stands on the shoulders of a people whose talents or achievements are particularly outstanding. They are committed to a people, Foundational Black Americans who, for almost 500 years, exemplified integrity, honesty, and decency in the face of overwhelming stress and oppression.

Certainly, they are using the understanding gained by critical thinkers who cared enough to sacrifice their selfishness so that we might make intellectual progress, which can have different connotations for Black people. Conscious Blacks are not only well-informed on issues of serious importance, they fortify themselves through the use of education, which gives them mental strength, or a stronger sense of moral commitment and encouragement. Conscious Blacks are also willing to actively engage the government and its policies.

Since most young Blacks refuse to attain a formal education, they often fail to trust collected facts and data about race matters. That skepticism makes it hard for them to accept historical accounts. The result is many young Black males have a limited understanding of history. In many cases, history has proven that a chronological account of past events is useful in resolving problems involving the current state of affairs. It's their skepticism that makes it hard for them to find viable solutions. This, I believe, is the reason why they will continue to endure the unnecessary process of trial-and-error.

Many young Blacks consider their elders to be illiterate. Others believe them to be out of touch with important constitutional changes that affect the younger generation. Thus, if they cannot trust their elders to educate them on important matters concerning the current state of affairs, and they don't, then they will surely refuse to attain information given to them by Whites. Regardless of the accuracy of this information, one thing I know for certain and two things for sure: lack of trust is the very reason why young Black males refuse to learn from White people. For the person who is *woke* to the situation of protesting, the struggle continues.

Still, we have a serious problem among Blacks. Blacks from the younger generation refuse to learn about their past. The sad fact is a lot of the richness acquired from Black history is passed down through oral and written tradition. Why is it so important to maintain? George Santayana said it best! "Those who forget the past are condemned to repeat it." And we have, once again, found ourselves in a similar situation that our elders confronted and readily resolved.

Blacks are back at it, protesting for justice in streets across the country. The problem I have with that is they're making the same mistakes made by our elders during the Civil Rights era. So, what's wrong with that, you ask? People have to learn, don't they? Indeed, people have to learn. That much is true. But the reason why societies record history is so later generations can learn from past mistakes. If only young Blacks would learn how to utilize historical events much like a battle plan, then they could gain a strategic advantage in helping forward their cause. By this I mean young Blacks should become skilled at resolving today's problems by learning from past mistakes. Blacks, as a people, must learn to educate themselves be it by way of formal or informal education.

A Perception Of Aggression

Whites often consider young Blacks to be aggressive. They believe that protesting is a way for them to express their aggression. Coupled with the belief that Blacks do not particularly care for Whites, many feel intimidated whenever young Black males are present. For this reason, Whites believe that Black masculinity is toxic. The fact that young Black males often take pride in their masculinity poses considerable problems for Whites.

While there is nothing wrong about taking pride in their masculinity, Whites consequently stigmatize them by denigrating emotions young Blacks comfortably express while engaged in daily interactions. They say their masculinity is detrimental to others thus calling on Black males to be subservient, quiet, or submissive to White male dominance.

The fact that they call Black male pride toxic masculinity tells me they are threatened by the courage and commitment of Black males. For that reason, Blacks are consciously rejecting the qualities of dominant society. They refuse to accept, agree to, believe in, or make use of any activities that equate to them acting White, thus being feminine. Formal education, church, theater and drama, even formal English, those activities conventionally belonging to Whites regardless of their mainstream qualities, are considered to be feminine to young Black males.

Blacks know they are not liked or respected by Whites. They understand that the discontent Whites have for them is largely due to differences in appearance. So, young Blacks make a concerted effort to not follow the etiquettes and mannerisms of dominant society. In this way, not-learning is a deliberate response made by a people who expect or have a right to expect love, kindness, and friendship. It may seem tacit and disabling to most people. Heck, I've often said Black people cannot respond intelligently to racism. They can only "react" to it. So I will correct my statement here. The act of purposely not learning, to not follow the rules and conventions governing correct or polite behavior in society or in specific social or professional situations is, in my opinion, a clever way to respond when dealing with an antagonistic force hostile to the idea of change.

If you still think Blacks are reacting to racism, remember how South Africans shutdown the South African government during apartheid. They boycotted their school system. Their deliberate actions forced the world to make an assessment of their personal worth. Thus, to respond intelligently to racism, one has to act in extreme ways. Yet, a third example that goes far beyond what's reasonable or conventional is the decision to adopt the term "real nigga."

Have you ever heard the phrase "turn a frown upside down?" It means to make someone happy after they show sadness. Well, that's what Black people often do for themselves and others. I mean, they have a tendency to make the best use of their tragic situation. For example, Whites assigned Black people to the labeled nigger. They've been saddled with that stigma ever since the period of chattel slavery. After a few modifications and changes, Blacks learned to use it as a term of endearment.

The preferred term used by young Black males today is "real nigga." It's a part of Black Vernacular speech. As slang, it is a casual, vivid, and racy term that replaces Standard English. Often short-lived, and usually considered unsuitable for formal contexts, it departs from the word usage nigger, a derogatory word used to berate Black people. Now, the word nigger derives from the derogatory word Negro, which is dated and offensive.

Young Black males use the term "real nigga" as a simple means to verify someone who is genuine or original. In embracing it, Blacks change the dominant view that they are socially unacceptable. It's also their way of shaming Whites by reminding them of their hypocrisy. In fact, the term now offends dominant society. What that tells me is that Black people fully embraced a negative stigma in an effort to heal themselves from the shame or disgrace attached to it. In this way, repeated use of the term acts as a constant reminder to White people that they are the main problem source in the lives of our most vulnerable. The fact that Whites cannot speak it, ever, also says Black people have taken a stance against the violent history of White supremacy.

Dually noted: It is important for you to understand that the word Negro is dated and offensive. It is a gross mischaracterization of Black people. It implies that life for Blacks (Africans, if you will) began in the sub-Saharan region of Africa, areas today known as Nigeria and the Niger Congo. The word sub-Sahara is also a misnomer. But, I digress! Fact of the matter is evolution began simultaneously in three separate and distinct locations in Africa. Hence, Black historians prefer to use the term Africoid or Akaloid or, perhaps, Akeloid, deriving its name from Alkebulan, the oldest known name of Africa.

Blacks from the younger generation have to learn the importance of education. It is a useful tool that can help make them less susceptible to vulnerability. This matter should be of the highest importance if they are to take back, keep, and develop their humanity. So when the opportunity does come, they will better understand their true sense of purpose in life.

What We Can Do To Resolve It

What we can do to resolve unconsciousness among Black Americans is encourage greater awareness. By encouraging a greater sense of awareness, we keep people well-informed about what is going on in the world or about the latest cultural developments. For Blacks who continue to put personal concerns and interests before those of others, we can pressure them to end their self-serving values. The more people achieve awareness, the more vigilant they become. They become especially guarded against those who pose a threat to our most vulnerable.

The formation of the US Green Party is one such example. Its members continue to function at the grassroots of socialism to address many concerns that plaque our most vulnerable. The Green Party was formed in 1984 by people who became aware that they were supporting political parties that held self-serving values. Its members are ready to put the general good, needs, or interests of others first. They appear to be attuned to the latest problems surrounding this country and our world. Climate change, corporate greed, mass incarceration, and endless wars, various problems in need of political attention, yet, are not listed as priorities on the political agenda of our nation's leaders. The Green Party keeps people well-informed and works as an alternative to politics that support the two parties of War and Wall Street.

We can also learn to admit that conscious Blacks and those *woke* aren't too different in term of their goals. One of their main goals in life is to reach full equality under the law. We even have similar ways to accomplish these goals. Open protest, seminars, and piece rallies are the means to achieving a healthy end. In fact, the only noticeable difference is in their willingness to learn. *Woke* Blacks will often reject information if recorded by historically White institutions. Conscious-minded Blacks will scrutinize the information before making their decision. They tend to be attuned to cultural problems that many of us find perplexing. Our ideals of freedom, democracy, and equality are complicated issues but approachable because of them. Both conscious Blacks and those *woke* refuse to accept a choice limited by a government ruled under the authority of the Oligarchy.

In this chapter, we focused extensively on two of awareness' most important mental states: unconsciousness and consciousness. In the final chapter, we will explore more on the end results of consciousness, given the arrival of your true identity.

Chapter 7
Arriving At Your True Identity

Refusing to Learn

It is a great shock at the age of five or six to find that in a world of Gary
Coopers you are the Indian.

James Baldwin (1924 – 1987)

James Baldwin once remarked, "An identity would seem to be arrived at by the way in which the person faces and uses his experience." Okay; what Baldwin said appears to be true. However, it doesn't seem to explain how people arrive when they refuse to learn. Their demeanor seems to detract from the entire concept of arriving.

As odd as it may seem, people who refuse to learn have, in many ways, a greater advantage. They are ready and willing to seek out the new, especially something like finding their true identity. It's the main reason why so many of them voluntarily withdraw from mainstream society so early in life. They're not trying to overcome obstacles or remove barriers just to have their hopes and aspirations devastated by the very people who oppressed them. They're not going to create a persona just to fit-in, either, especially when that image contradicts their morals or values. So, for them, what you see is what you get!

In contrast, it may be hard for the average Black person to break from society. The hustle and bustle of daily living can create responsibilities that obligate them. In many instances, they choose to delay their decision to break from society until the last possible moment. Mortgage, car note, family, and a career can compel people to remain complacent as a legal or moral duty. In actuality, its how they choose to address and then handle their decision that determines who they are, what they're all about, and where they're headed in life. Thus, who you are to become is decided in one defining moment.

A Defining Moment

There will come a time in your life when you have to reach a decision. It is at that defining moment when a significant change or development occurs or a decision is reached. How you cope with that decision can mark the beginning of a completely new, and usually better, stage of development in your life. When we think about how people rise above their circumstances, two important questions arise: Have they arrived at their true identity? And, how can we tell if they truly arrived at their true identity?

There are many ways you can tell when someone has arrived at their true identity. Think about those who do arrived at their true identity. Now think about your qualities or values. Consider your set of characteristics, for example. Do you perceive your personal qualities to be important or useful? Does your demeanor match your persona? How about vice versa? We can see how people who refuse to learn may not fit the bill. But make no mistakes about it, many of them already arrived, but in their own way. Fact of the matter is many people arrive at their true identity. But, they may vary in their orientation toward it, each having their own sense of personal direction.

A Sense Of Personal Direction

There is nothing more life-affirming than having a sense of personal direction. There aren't too many gratifying experiences in life. Those who refuse to learn may not appear to have a good understanding of the concept. But, one can never tell. "He's a nice guy, but seems to lack a sense of direction," an observer might notice. The young man, however, appears to be more invested in matters of self-interest, which gives him a sense of personal direction. The observer may never notice. Who's to say whether one person or group has a monopoly on such matters? Perhaps, society determines who is purposeful or lacking or which matters are meaningful.

Young Black males have been overlooked or forgotten by society simply because they appear to be nonconforming. They can make the argument that society never embraced them. At no point in US history has there been a campaign to encourage a more perfect union between Whites and Blacks. Yet, many Black people rise above their circumstances to achieve a life that is meaningful or purposeful.

There are Black people who reach a point where they are ready to withdraw from society. Many feel like it's the only way if they are to have any hope of maintaining a sense of personal direction. Consider James Baldwin, for example. James Arthur Baldwin was born and raised in Harlem, New York, NY. The stepchild of a Baptist preacher, David Baldwin, James found solace in community libraries. It was there he would discover his passion for literary writing. Most of his teachers considered James to be gifted. And in 1937, he proved them right, when at the tender age of 13, James submitted his first article titled *Harlem: Then and Now*. He published it in his school's magazine, The Douglass Pilot.

Disspite the fact that dominant society wanted to maintain their traditional way of life because they desire an independent existence, at the age of 23, Baldwin left America. He was determined to not limit his writing talents to the literary title of Negro author or author of Negro literature. While living abroad in Paris, Baldwin would further his writing talents where he wrote passionate and thought-provoking literature on the topic of race in America. His style of writing included novels, essays, and plays.

Baldwin would come to be known as an intellectual. Even without formal education, his proof, most of it independent proof, came largely from his literary works. Baldwin, a self-styled man, would proclaim his place in global history as a world renowned author and literary genius, best known for his novels, plays, essays, poems, and his commitment to political activism.

Baldwin's journey showed that young Blacks no longer have to endure adversity. They can find a way to avoid opposition imposed by oppressive laws without actually breaking any. Baldwin persevered over his adversities by circumventing his oppressors. Still, there are people who refuse to learn (in Baldwin's case, he refused to learn from his oppressors). They separate themselves from the cultural mainstream. Yet, they manage to preserve their integrity. The fact that many manage to find a sense of direction in mediocrity (Baldwin refused it) shows Blacks are capable of rising above their circumstances no matter what the situation might be.

Consider young Black males, many of whom join the military to avoid their immediate circumstances. They rise above oppressive conditions to become military leaders. Colin Powell became a four-star general in the United States Army. He later became the first African American Secretary of State. Even Blacks who join the Nation of Islam rise to become men of great distinction.

The Civil Rights Era inspired many young Black males to join the Nation of Islam, for example. It was the Honorable Elijah Muhammad who taught Black Americans their history. Over the years, many Blacks would find a sense of personal direction through his teachings. There was also an unlikely character who would rise above his circumstance to become a world-renowned religious leader. Louis Eugene Walcott would become the honorable Louis Abdul Farrakhan who would later succeed his predecessor the Honorable Elijah Muhammad. The two religious leaders were, at one point in history, unlikely to meet with success, Elijah Muhammad being a sharecropper and Minister Farrakhan coming from the Bronx, New York.

Today, both gentlemen are greatly admired, Muhammad deceased since 1975. As religious leaders, they exceeded National expectations by going beyond our ability to deal with or understand matters that overload our adaptability. Many people model themselves after our nation's leaders. Many of our leaders are excellent examples of humanity who deserve to be imitated. They exemplify all the qualities we hope to embody.

People personify the image of our nation's leaders in the hope of making similar contributions or resembling something close to their achievements on a smaller scale. In this way, the idea of assuming an important role in society is immensely gratifying. However, it is enough to cause problems, especially from people who pretend to be someone else in order to deceive. Here, we can say that arriving at your *true identity* occurs when your personal qualities match your assumed identity, social role, or persona.

Forced Or Overly Clever:
Living Vicariously Through
An Assumed Identity

The mere thought of people arriving at their true identity can predispose others to behave in vicarious ways. People often role-play or mimic those they most admire in an effort to better understand how they arrived at their true identity.

Church-going folk often admire pastors for their charisma and self-determination. As such, they often seek direct spiritual experiences during Christian worship. They look for inspired and ecstatic experiences such as healing, prophecy, and speaking in tongues in order to better understand the level of knowledge their pastors have to offer. They conduct life in a way that brings hope and admiration to their own determination. We then say they have a special calling. They are more often mimicking what the admired profess and what they would like to believe in or value. There is hope for those who seek the righteous path; but, their ambitions often seem forced or overly clever.

People often mimic other members of society who are regarded as significant or possessing special qualities. Why? They prefer to be more like them. They often feel that other people have lifestyles that are more meaningful or more significant than their own. So they assume the identity or role of the person who is most admired. The hope is for them to create an image most liked the admired. If they do, the projected image would be so impressionable that people will come to admire them or treat them the same as, or greater than, those most admire.

There is a concept that originated in Jungian psychology, a psychoanalysis that speaks to the image of character and personality people would like to show the outside world. A *persona* is Carl Jung's idea of an identity or role that someone assumes to conceal the person's true nature. In Jungian theory, the persona they project to the outside world fails to match their personal characteristics. In this book, we venture further by saying, in many cases, people create personas not to hide who they are from the outside world but to show the world who they'd like to become.

Many people create personas. Perhaps, the best example was characterized in a poem written by Paul Lawrence Dunbar. In his American classic, *We Wear the*

Mask, Dunbar describes how Black people are compelled by their compassion for humanity in order to conceal or disguise their feelings so as to coexist with their oppressors. In the poem, he refers to the cheerful facial expressions of happy-go-lucky Negros as a necessary cover to prevent others from feeling or sharing in their emotional pain.

It wasn't until young Blacks actively engaged in the Civil Rights movement that many would come to realize their elders created personas not in fear but to endure. Their unselfish commitment to suffering taught younger generations of Blacks that no one is above sacrifice. From that point onward, many Blacks began to understand that the need to serve a greater purpose benefited not only them but future generations. It was probably that defining moment when young Black activists began arriving at their true identity. They would come to learn that arriving at their true identity relied on people who paved the way for them to succeed.

The Dangers Of Arriving

Arriving at your true identity can present certain dangers. It often comes in response to the way you perform in spite of your circumstances. For example, Eugene Jacques Bullard was born Eugene James Bullard. Bullard became the first Black American military pilot in global history in spite US policies, restricting Blacks from flying. Bullard was one of a few Black combat pilots who flew for France during World War I.

Another example includes the American civil rights leader Medgar Evers, a young Black man who joined the Civil Rights movement in spite of the dangers of participating in protest demonstrations. Medgar, a prior service member and no stranger to violence, was shot to death by white supremacist Byron De La Beckwith in the driveway outside of his home in Jackson, Mississippi. Arriving at your true identity is not like finding your niche, which is an activity that best suits your talents and personality. It's more like finding a sense of personal direction. It is said to be like coming into your own, manning up, or coming into personhood.

Arriving at your true identity occurs not because someone wills it. But because of your own abilities and efforts, you rise above your circumstances to become who you are. That's not to say you, as a person, will never receive help along the way. Being provided with advice, direction, or other guidance will comfort you in your journey. It can even come from someone who made it easier or possible for you to experience an impactful moment in a way no one person can do alone.

Black people are constantly rising above their circumstances. As an oppressed identity group, it doesn't benefit them to play the role of victim. For example, society is visibly upset by Blacks who constantly complain about their circumstances with the apparent hopes of eliciting sympathy from strangers and others. Whites claim that Blacks often complain about their living conditions even though they apparently created it though crime, drug use, neglect, and abandonment of their own communities.

And although it appears to be true of Blacks, I assure you, it is not the case.

Since 1967, Blacks have been a source of great worry, stress, or trouble for their oppressors. When Black people argue their oppression, for example, dominant society frequently complains that Blacks, who are apparent victims of their own circumstances, will play the race card to win an advantage. The complaint is that Black people will use the issue of race in a debate or heated argument just to win an advantage.

Black people are often accused of playing the race card. However, when they do play it, it's simply to make their point perfectly clear, not to win an advantage. Although winning an advantage often comes when you make a point perfectly clear, I assure you, there are no rewards or benefits for Black people when they are repeatedly exploited, oppressed, or publicly humiliated, especially by the Oligarchy who seek to control them for their own benefit. That's not to say Blacks aren't victims of their circumstances. In fact, quite a few Blacks are. But, their circumstances were created by the Oligarchy. Hence lies the motivation needed to effect change in their lives.

For Black people, arguing their oppression is necessary to arrive at their true identity. To succeed or fail depending on the circumstances is crucial. Why? Their oppressors are politically, financially, and socially powerful people who, together, govern the nation often for their own benefit. As such, they could take a tough stance against Black people. If so, Blacks could be subjected to dominating influences that take away their freedom and independence. The sudden loss of sovereignty could complicate their efforts to arrive at their true identity. Thus, Blacks have to be persuasive when arguing their rights in spite of resistance to the idea.

To date, their oppressors continue to have immense political power wielded by large corporations. These corporations are controlled largely by special interest groups. Unfortunately, special interests are controlled by a collective. This collective is known as the Oligarchy. Sadly, and although it's been a long, arduous process, with the amount of racial tension and hostility brewing in the nation, Blacks may never arrive at their true identity, not as a race, never individually.

Measured By What Is Often Ignored Or Take For Granted

As Blacks arrive at their true identity, they learn to enjoy or appreciate what is often ignored or taken for granted. This mental state is exactly why people who refuse to learn find a sense of personal direction in mediocrity. Here, we are interested in how Black people arrive at their true identity and what personal qualities help them to develop it. Throughout this section and the rest of the chapter, we will continue our discussion on arriving at your true identity. Again, your *true identity* occurs when your personal qualities match your assumed identity, social role, or persona.

The Finer Things In Life

For some people, the finer things in life refer to material wealth and object possessions. For the sake of understanding your true identity and the intended purpose of this book, *the finer things in life* refers to someone who developed spiritual or intellectual values and enjoys or appreciates what people often ignore or take for granted.

We often take for granted precious reminders and moments. Friendships and loved ones are often taken for granted. Even when the act is unintentional or caused by a lack of knowledge, it shows a sense of selfishness. In this case, there are still elements of your identity that believe your personal needs and wishes are more important than other people.

For Black people, you haven't arrived until you've reached a certain amount of appreciation for life. One of the first things that happen when arriving at your true identity is you begin to challenge beliefs that everyone else takes for granted. This important mental progression enhances your ability for doing well. It is here, at this point in time, your mind will provide you with a unique opportunity to stimulate your intellectual growth. You will develop a sound and open-minded understanding of life to include awareness or sensitivity to important issues. Such growth has a profound impact not just on your perception but those in your surrounding environment. From that point onward, you will come to enjoy or appreciate what people often ignore or take for granted.

There is a certain level of confidence also associated with arriving at your true identity. For example, another thing that happens to you is the belief in your own abilities. You may come to learn that your personal attributes give you an added advantage in daily life. You may also find that your attributes have more value or greater benefit, or that your values bring you greater advantage. Others may also start to believe in or trust your ability to act in a proper, trustworthy, or reliable manner. You will also begin to develop mutually beneficial relationships with other cultures, groups, or members of society.

That being said, there's no better feeling than arriving at your true identity. It's the feeling of arriving that is awe inspiring. If it could be characterized, arriving would feel like finding your sense of direction, that feeling of having a definite goal or purpose. As such, arriving is the perfect embodiment of our hopes, dreams, and aspirations. Case in point, Dr. Cornel Ronald West:

Dr. Cornel West is an American philosopher, political activist, and democratic intellectual. As an intellectual, he is passionate about communicating with people from various social spheres. His hope is to keep alive the legacy of Martin Luther King, Jr. The two shared a vision: to tell the truth and bear witness to love and justice.

Dr. Cornel West is a man of great distinction who had the dubious distinction of being called a prophet. He came into his own during the first ten years as one of the most prophetic intellectuals of our times. But, it would be his book Race Matters that catapulted him to the level of intellectual. Before then, he was known as an upcoming and extremely talented speaker.

Dr. Cornel West or Cornel, as he likes to be called, wasn't always a bestselling author, activist, and intellectual, either. He did acknowledge he was a redeemed sinner with gangster proclivities. So then, how did Cornel overcome his adversities to become one of the most influential public intellectuals of our time? A lot of time and energy was invested into the brother; that how!

Cornel credited his upbringing to the teachings of his parents and community. The structure gave him the moral strength or encouragement to become a democratic intellectual. Long before arriving at Harvard, Princeton, and other prestigious collegiate institutions, his parents and community provided him with a certain soul-craft, which shaped and modified his soul or core being. From the sports arena of high school entertainment to family, church, and an entire network of community resources, his people were first responders to his personal crises.

Later, his philosophy would make it easy for him to understand the plight and predicament of humanity. He also had the ability to envision cultural problems people confronted nearly 30 years ahead of time, which he demonstrated in his book, Race Matters, first published in 1993-94. In addition, Cornel is an integrationist or activist who worked to maintain cultural integrity. Further, Cornel is a true democratic supporter who supported a cultural movement that promoted the rights of all people to become an integral part of the larger culture.

Cornel became the focus of public attention due to his outspoken views on race, culture, and the politics of gender. As a result, he arrived at his true identity relatively early in life. Until this day, Dr. West continues to share dialogue with a vast variety of publics.

Another public intellectual who embodied what it meant to arrive at your true identity was Dr. Claud Anderson. Dr. Anderson arrived at his true identity so long ago he retired early and turned all of his attention inward to help empower his own people. He refused to hold back from speaking to audiences in ways that would prevent them from being annoyed, hurt, or even riled. He even dedicated his reference books to Black people with the intention of teaching them how to reestablish independence in Black areas of American society.

Curiously, Dr. Anderson holds what many people considered to be separatist views. His views are surprising or revealing to many people. He always encourages Black people to reestablish their own communities. He believes that Black people needed to achieve sovereignty. In order for them to accomplish this feat, they will need to have their own economy, a code of conduct, and political independence in America. Even at the ripe old age of 85, Dr. Anderson continues to be ornery about racial integration.

Drs. Cornel West and Claud Anderson are men of great distinction. Both found their sense of purpose relatively early in life. Cornel fortified his knowledge with the truth and wisdom of past elders: Fannie Lou Hamer, Ida B. Wells-Barnett, and Ella Josephine Baker who understood that you couldn't engage in civil rights activism without engaging in human rights activism, and many more who understood the sacrifice. Dr. Anderson is a walking encyclopedia. In this way, both gentlemen present information so clearly true that it hardly ever needs to be restated. Still, they have very different approaches to problem-solving. The connection between their identities is said to be one of love and justice.

Both men come with tremendous insight. They have the ability to see clearly and intuitively into the nature of complex cultural problems that affected Blacks long before many people could understand their immediate dangers. Dr. West thoroughly believes in formal education. Dr. Anderson pushes for informal education. He truly believed that a formal education is the last activity Blacks should partake in. His main focus is the reestablishment of Black communities and any education that supported racial upheaval.

There is a take-a-way we can leave the reader. People arrive at their true identity at any time in life. But when they find their sense of purpose, they know they're on the right path. Perhaps every society has members who arrive at their true identity even though the people who arrive may vary in their orientation toward it. Regardless of how they arrive, there is a tendency to develop spiritual or intellectual values that allow them to enjoy or appreciate what most people ignore or take for granted: the need to love and respect other human beings.

In The Age Of White Supremacy

For Black people, life is complicated. Their history is fragmented. Their existence is tormented. The problem is they had their identity completely removed from them during slavery. Three hundred forty-six years later, they would argue their way out of systemic oppression, at least, to a degree. They have been putting together the pieces of their history ever since. However, the reason for their oppression is not that complicated.

In fact, it's not the least bit complicated! Neither White supremacy nor its motives are difficult to understand. White supremacy is a method of racial oppression. Its purpose is to subject a person or a people to harsh or cruel forms of domination. The objective is to allow its members to rule with endless boundaries. It has been the goal or desire of the Oligarchy to rule endlessly since its members landed on the shores of this great nation of ours. Make no mistake about it! Even when King James authorized the transcription of the King James Version Christian Bible, he was looking for ways to rule beyond the outer limits of his kingdom.

Arriving at your true identity can be especially dangerous in the age of White supremacy. New Jim Crow laws in the new millennium greatly impact the lives of Black Americans. Many of these laws were devised to keep Blacks oppressed or subservient. Politicians create new laws and regulate policies that discriminate against Blacks usually because Whites are prejudiced about race. Dominant society did its part to present itself a serious problem. For example, Donald Trump and the Republican Party gave the country Trump loyalists. He also gave America a group called "Republican In Name Only" or RINO's. In the same way, far-right media extremists known as Sharpie-gate reared its ugly xenophobic head just to introduce the concept of media racism.

Many of these cultural discrepancies come mainly from not having the same political views. Black people made great efforts over a period of time to become bipartisan, which has resulted in there being many disadvantages for Black people in America. In this way, Black people often have to push their own political agenda for equal rights. Although it continues to be an uphill struggle, they make significant progress in planning and organizing actions with the specific goal to raise awareness about race in contemporary America. They organize piece rallies and public speeches as well as marches and protest demonstrations with the intent to persuade the country to change its voting priorities. Blacks have been successful at each and every step in the political process to assure their sovereignty. In this way, they are distracted from arriving at their true identity.

Black people are so distracted by racial violence or hate-crimes that they haven't been able to arrive at their true identity. Freedom fighter, civil rights activist, Black Nationalist, and Pan-African are just a few social roles

Black people assume over long periods of time that become their individual personality or identity for life. Each one of these social roles requires personal qualities that might be considered offensive, especially when assuming rolls that conflict with mainstream values.

So you asked, how is it possible to be distracted by violence when it has been the catalyst behind this push for a truly independent identity? Heavy distracters result when Black people fail to share a similar outlook or viewpoint in life. Quite a few Blacks are torn between worldviews. Thanks to Donald Trump's political views, some continue to be undecided or unable to choose between political parties. Thus, if structural barriers to equality never existed, Blacks would be able to exercise free will and make independent choices without being subject to any undue restraints or restrictions.

It also happens when Black people experience discomfort, uneasiness, and fear of change. Many Blacks choose not to rock the proverbial boat on political issues. We call them conservative. They often relinquish their identity and then join the Republican Party, stating that right-winged political views better suit their political agenda. These are the people who would like to keep the state of affairs constant. They would also deny other Blacks opportunities to prevent them from gaining access to important resources if they lacked mainstream values. Such distractions work against the maintenance of cultural integrity as well as the struggle to achieve sovereignty, which is needed to arrive at their true identity. However, there has always been enough momentum to continue the push for a separate and distinct identity.

The fight to arrive at their true identity has always been in danger, though. How do we know that? Well, Blacks have always had to flight to establish racial equality in America. They've also had to organize a few Civil Rights movements; and, it continues to be an uphill battle. Some time ago, Black Lives Matter (#BLM) launched a global network in order to call to arms political allies to undertake the problem of racial inequality in America.

Black Lives Matter built enough momentum to catalyze other organizations across the nation and around the world. As a matter of fact, the BLM global network started the largest Black liberation struggle in global history. Yet, while it may help them to arrive at their true identity, many other Black people are so distracted by the struggle that they do not have enough momentum to find their own identity. In this way, Blacks have been diverted away from arriving at their true identity. Hence, they continue to be in danger of losing their identity. In a capsule, the dangers associated with reaching full equality have kept Blacks from thinking clearly or acting sensibly enough to arrive at their true identity. The question is are things changing; are times getting better?

What We Can Do To Resolve It

For once, there's not much we can do as there are no clear consensus arrived at or currently being taken into consideration to resolve the problem. However, might I suggest that instead of removing obstacles that hinder or prevent the arrival of the true Black identity, we should find a way to avoid impediments and barriers?

Realistically, obstacles are put in place to distract or interfere with Black people and their natural progression. It also takes their attention away from succeeding in daily life. As for barriers, well, that's just a blockade of angry law makers who are upset over a few Blacks who managed to succeed in spite of government efforts to block their progression. With this understanding, Black people need not be drawn into any activities that divert their attention away from progress. Therefore, they need a planned course of action.

But first, Blacks need to understand that the best available resources used to combat oppression can be found by looking within. What they should not do is wait on strangers and others to pick up and fight their battles. It's been fun and quite educational to watch White people ally in protest of racism and White supremacy. Hell, I've even said, and I've been saying this since 1996, Black people should set out the next Civil Rights movement and let White people have at it if they are to earn our respect. Truth of the matter is White people should not have to fight battles for Black people. Certainly, they can ally. Heck, I recommend it! So, a good solution to our problem requires Black people to look at their situation realistically.

The one problem Blacks have is accepting the hardcore truth: Black people's problem in America is that White people have a problem with Black folk. If they can accept that realization, then Blacks can learn to look ahead and plan for the future; and here comes a solution. Blacks should anticipate and counter any plans their oppressors may have that continue Black oppression.

Second, Black people need to continue doing what's been done lately. That is to say, they need to continue showing admiration and consideration for their own people. In this way, they can focus immediate attention on group interests, especially when learning how to place health and wellness before those of other people. Simply said, you have to first learn how to help yourself before you can help someone else in need.

There are many activist groups emerging everyday that can teach Black people how to become independent and self-sustaining. In fact, momentum is building and Blacks are soon to have a movement for national independence. Now that doesn't mean Blacks can't aid others in their struggle from time-to-time. It simply means there is much work to be done at home.

What young Blacks need to understand is that when you lose the ability to fend for yourself, it creates a situation or period in which life becomes very uncertain, difficult, or painful, especially a time when action must be taken to avoid complete disaster or breakdown, which you may choose to call a preventable moment against spiritual blackout. Even the church can be taken into consideration when fighting against spiritual blackout as it involves a loss of morals, values, and integrity from the apparent unfairness or unreasonableness of their situation. The church has been known to help young Blacks arrive at their true identity. Case in point: Drs. Cornel West, Eric M. Dyson, Martin Luther King, Jr., Coretta Scott King, and others belonging to that group.

Last, and a major challenge, is to prevent the fire the next time. James Baldwin took this passage from the Christian Bible. It was a message God gave Noah. God sent Noah a sign in the form of a rainbow. It was interpreted as a warning, saying if we, as a civilization, fail to succeed in bettering our situation or adhering to change, there will be no more destroying earth by water; there will be fire the next time. In this way, it is clearly evident that dominant society would like to keep Black people locked into a permanent underclass. If they get their way, Blacks may not get another chance to progress or succeed in American society, ever! To reiterate my point, they will be completely teased apart from the cultural mainstream, forced into a permanent underclass not just in American society but globally. And for that reason, there will be hell to pay.

We've just witnessed a spiritual blackout and imperial meltdown of mainstream values and core problems with our political system thanks-speed to Donald J. Trump. Regardless of our situation in America, we need to determine whether Blacks will be given the same or equal opportunities afforded Whites. Or was that moment of xenophobic frenzy witnessed on January 6, 2021, simply a sign of times to come?

Black people in America have a need to establish their own identity. Yet, there are many obstacles and barriers set in place to prevent them from succeeding.

Black men (increasingly Black women) are more likely than White men to receive prison confinement after grade school for crimes of minor offenses. Such catastrophes are responsible for sudden and violent changes in society. For example, White police abuse and greater attacks on the integrity of Black folk is why they protest against racial inequality and social injustice. It's also why White people are at odds with themselves. It is a direct response to undermining the credibility and possibility of Black folk in America.

There needs to be a reconciliation to end conflict and tension between disputing groups in order to create healthy and productive change in American society. Heck, it necessary for the establishment of healthy intergroup relations.

If we don't learn to develop empathy and compassion for one another, it won't be Trump loyalists who rain on America's parade. It will be fire the next time.

Chapter 7 is the last of 7 chapters from the book Refusing to Learn: Really, How Dumb Do You Think I Am? It was intended to orient you and other readers. Many unanswered questions about arriving at your true identity remain. However, the chapter was designed to encourage you on your journey to greater awareness and independence. You have to admit, it does provide a sense of direction that should make your journey more enjoyable and humane. What could be more important to anyone than this book's main objective: to bring into consideration an important sociocultural problem not uttered or talked about in today's society, even though it's often thought about.

One of the most important themes of Refusing to Learn has been the psychology of young Black males who are forced to live in a society that functions under the double standard of White supremacy. Following this chapter, you will find an Epilogue that focuses on your essential self.

Epilogue
Your Essential Self

> If there is no struggle, there is no progress.
>
> Frederick Douglass (Unknown - 1895)

White people often ask shattering questions like, "What's going to happen to Black people if their circumstances become increasingly worse?" Well, they will pick up the torch and continue the struggle of course. But, that's just what they are afraid of! White people have been trying to control the Black population ever since they realized Blacks were the competition.

The Nature Of Your Essential Self

Your essential self is what we refer to as personal attributions or values. It can be your complete and individual identity or personal qualities that, essentially, characterize your personality, especially ones that society recognizes as belonging specifically to you as an individual and with which there is a sense of ease. In fact, your *essential self* is made up of defining qualities that make you who you are.

Maintaining Your Essential Self

The ultimate goal of Black folk is to maintain their essential self. The idea is to withdrawal from the larger culture to achieve independence. The goal is to not become separatists like the Bull Connor's and James Strom Thurmond's of America. The goal and intended purpose of their self-imposed withdrawal is to develop a complete and independent identity so they can get in touch with their essential selves. Sacrifices will have to be made. Many people will put their lives on hold, which means they may lose essential aspects of themselves.

But, there is a seemingly tricky question that needs to be addressed. And, it sounds like a paradox. How do Black people rekindle or maintain essential aspects of them when they're seeking out a new identity? True, sacrifices must be made if they are to find their own way in life. But, does that really mean they have to lose important aspects of their essential self just to make it happen?

The answer is no! It is unnecessary to lose who you are even in the name of peace. Now that doesn't mean people haven't lost the understanding of who they are in an effort to avow their identity. So, the next question becomes, how do they resolve that problem? The idea is to achieve a personal balance between group activities and your self-interests. Don't worry! There will be enough people around to help you create the proper balance. Proper balance usually involves staying active with Afrocentric activities and the current state of affairs or, even, personal activities of interests. It is often referred to as maintaining your spiritual or intellectual values.

How are Black people going to maintain their essential self, especially when society fails to respect their avowed identity? As Blacks gain freedom from oppression, dominant society will have to come to terms with Blacks and their ability or right to make their own decisions without interference from their oppressors. It's a matter of gaining confidence in their independence. Blacks will begin developing workable strategies to continue or keep their self-interests in existence despite the pressures of change.

Dominant society will also have to change. America is failing as a nation due to its refusal to change. It's government refuses to adapt to the pressures of change whereas societies that do change learn how to survive. Politicians create laws that displace Black people with increasing regularity. The types of laws available continue to shift consideration from Blacks to Hispanics, which accounts for the constant effort to berate Black people. In addition, White Americans are increasingly becoming hate-filled. As a result, their survivability in America may rest on the ability to relate to immigrants who continue to immigrate into the country. Further, Blacks are refusing to learn from Whites in fear of being miseducated or misinformed, which could very well push them into a permanent underclass.

How do Black people arrive under such circumstances? Many laws are becoming more complex and more discriminatory. As more laws are created to protect dominant society, Black people as such Jamaicans, Haitians, and Black Americans face greater uncertainty. That is, more of them believe they are being locked out of the cultural mainstream because of a growing demand to replace Black competition with Hispanic labor. Many Black people believe that in the future, their place in American society may depend on an executive order issued by the President of the United States.

Throughout its continued history, America has not had an admirable record where Blacks have been concerned or where citizens of the world become involved. The new millennium represents an important passage in history where members of dominant society can make important contributions to achieving equality for Black Americans. White people not only need to improve their demeanor toward Black Americans but, as indicated throughout previous chapters, they also need to show more consideration for their health and wellness.

Use this book to improve your understanding of cultural problems that affect how Black people cope under the overwhelming stress of oppression and consider advocating racial equality to improve not only the lives of Black people but people from every walk of life: Native American, Eskimo, Asian, Hispanics, Arabian, and those belonging to this group, and by allying through support, advocate services, open protest, and other forms of interventions and considerations.

References

Anonymous (2021). <u>Resurrection City</u>. National Park Service U.S. Department of the Interior. Website. [Online] Available: https://www.nps.gov/articles/resurrection-city.htm

Anonymous. (2020). <u>Oligarchy</u>. Search Engine. [Online] Available: www.google.com

Alexander, M. (2012). <u>The New Jim Crow: Mass Incarceration in the Age of Colorblindness</u>. New York, NY. The New Press.

Anderson, C. (2018). <u>White Rage: The Unspoken Truth of Our Nation's Divide</u>. Social Media. [Online] Available: https://www.youtube.com/watch?v=YBYUET24K1c

Anderson, C. (2019). Dr. Claud Anderson Discusses America's Race Based Society, PowerNomics + More. The Breakfast Club Power 105.1. [Online] Available: https://www.youtube.com/watch?v=fW39KOf_f04&t=3571s

Baldwin, J. (1992). <u>The Fire The Next Time</u>. Reissue Edition. Vintage International: www.vintagebooks.com

DeGruy, J. (2020). <u>2011 Building Bridges – Keynote</u>.

Alabama State University. Public Lecture [Online] Available. https://www.youtube.com/watch?v= pact4iJLlog

DeGruy, J. (2020). Black History Convocation 2020 with Dr. Joy DeGruy. Public Lecture. Alabama State University. Lecture [Online] Available. https://www.youtube.com/ watch?v=pact4iJLlog

Dovidio, J. F. and Gaertner, S. L. (Eds.). (1986). Prejudice, Discrimination, and Racism. New York: Academic Press.

Garza, A. Cullors, P. Tometi. O. (2013). Black Lives Matter. Social Movement. [Online] Available: https://blacklivesmatter.com/

Hollie, S. (March 24, 2009). The (Mis)Education of Black Boys. Public Lecture. Social Media [Online] Available: https://www.youtube.com/watch?v= 7KyFWKnsnQQ

Hollie, S. (2017). Culturally and Linguistically Responsive Teaching and Learning: Classroom Practices for Student Success, Grades. (2nd Ed.). Huntington Beach, CA: Shell Education

Jones, J. M. (1996). Prejudice and Racism. (2nd Ed.) Columbus, OH: McGraw-Hill.

Kaufman, P. (2016). Why Some Students Refuse to Learn. Blog [Online] Available: https://www.everydaysociologyblog.com/2016/01/ why-some-students-refuse-to-learn.html

King, M. L. (1965). Creative Maladjustment, UCLA: UCLA Communications Studies Department. Social Media. [Online] Available: https://www.youtube.com/watch?v=t2vD1skiz80

King, M. L. (1965). Creative Maladjustment. International Association for the Advancement of Creative Maladjustment: Social Media. [Online] Available: https:// www.youtube.com/watch?v=rmF3XiQ WUnM

Kohl, H. (1993). I won't learn from you: And Other Thoughts on Creative Maladjustment. New York, NY. The New Press.

Lynch M. (2020) A Guide to Ending the Crisis Among Young Black Males. [Online] Available: https://www.theedadvocate.org/guide-ending-crisis-among-young-black-males/

McGuire, B. C. (2019). The Ignoble Paradox of Man. (Revised Ed.) Kindle Direct Publishing, Indie Publishing. [Online] Available: www.amazon.com

McGuire, B. C. (2020). The Color of Our Souls. Kindle

Direct Publishing, Indie Publishing. [Online] Available: www.amazon.com

McGuire, B. C. (2020). <u>The Great Divide: The Social and Cultural Context of Inequality</u>. (First Ed.) Kindle Direct Publishing. Indie Publishing. [Online] Available: www.amazon.com

Rose, Tricia, (2017). <u>How Structural Racism Works</u>. Social Media. [Online] Available: https://www.youtube.com/ watch?v=bC3TWx9IOUE

Rothman, R. A. (1999). <u>Inequality and Stratification: Race, Class, and Gender</u>. (3rd Ed.). Upper Saddle River, New Jersey: Prentice Hall.

Schaefer, R. T. (2005). <u>Race and Ethnicity in the United States</u>. (3rd Ed.). Upper Saddle River, New Jersey: Prentice Hall.

Sears, D. O. (1987). <u>Symbolic Racism</u>. In P. Kitz & D. Taylor (Eds.), Towards the Elimination of Racism: Profile in Controversy. New York: Plenum.

West, C. (2017). <u>Race Matters</u>: Twenty-fifth Anniversary Edition. Beacon Press. Boston, MA.

West, C. (2018). <u>Spiritual Blackout, Imperial Meltdown,</u>

<u>Prophetic Fightback</u>. Public Lecture. Askwith Forum: https://www.youtube.com/results?sp=mAEB&search_query=cornel+west+spiritual+black out

Woodson, C. G. (2006). The Mis-Education Of The Negro. Charlotte, NC: Khalifah's Books.

www.ingramcontent.com/pod-product-compliance
Lightning Source LLC
Chambersburg PA
CBHW070116260726
48658CB00001B/125